Tony Flannery CSsR

The Death of Religious Life?

D1550227

the columba press

First published in 1997 by
the columba press
55a Spruce Avenue, Stillorgan Industrial Park
Blackrock, Co Dublin

Cover by Bill Bolger
Origination by The Columba Press
Printed in Ireland by Colour Books Ltd, Dublin

ISBN 1 85607 198 7

Contents

CHAPTER 1

Products of our time

On a small farm in the fifties, saving the hay was the major task of the year. My father, who was normally a placid, almost timid type of man, took on a new personality when the hay was cut. He became frenetic, so that none of us had any peace while it lay on the ground. In fact, the hay dominated the whole summer. Weather forecasts were listened to very closely, and the time to cut each field was carefully decided. John Noone, who was the man who usually came to cut our hay, was summoned when the time was right, and was greatly abused if he didn't come promptly. He was corner back on the local hurling team, and when he came in for the meal after knocking the field of hay, the prospects for the championship were discussed at length. In those days we in Galway did not even talk about the county team. They were not worth serious consideration. Club hurling was all, and our lives revolved around it. Indeed it was a simple and uncomplicated life we lived. Work on the family farm, school and sport were what absorbed us. Social life was restricted as much by the absence of transport as by the strict family mores in which many of us grew up. Rural electrification had only just arrived, and the communications media were limited to the daily paper, and a fairly primitive form of radio. The outside world had little enough opportunity to influence our lives, and to challenge the accepted values of the society.

These values were largely controlled by the church. I clearly remember one summer in my middle teens saving the hay with my father. We were turning the swaths with pitchforks, a slow and tedious job, always done with one eye at the sky to see when the next rain was due to arrive. We were discussing my future. I, the youngest in the family, was in the junior seminary of a religious congregation, and my two older brothers had already advanced to the major seminary. I was telling my father that I intended to follow them. He was pleased. I remember the feeling of well-being I had during that conversation. There was a sense of a very coherent world, with a clear and widely accepted value system, and that what I had chosen to do with my life was a good and worthwhile thing. There was a consciousness of it also being a sacrificial thing, but that did not impinge too strongly on me at the time.

There was, instead, a certain status about becoming a religious. It set one apart. (At that stage in my life, in my youthful innocence, I thought that being set apart was a desirable thing!) It gave promise of a good education, an exciting life, with the possibility of travel. Our education at the time had strongly inculcated into us the value of service, and this was the ultimate service – to give your life completely in the service of others, to do the greatest thing of all for them, to save their souls. And in the process to guarantee your own salvation – that 'crown of glory' which even we in the junior seminary were regularly told would await those who lived and died faithfully in the congregation. How easy it all sounded then, and how right! Faith in God was everything, and it was part of the air that we breathed. This life was only a brief trial, a preparation for eternal life, and 'what does it profit a man…' was often pounded into our young heads in the local church. Looking back, it is amazing that nobody, neither my parents nor the authorities in the school or the order I was joining, seemed to see anything unusual in three brothers from a sheltered background joining the order and wanting to be priests, or suggested to me that I might have been just following their lead, or that I should take some time out before making a decision. But in that society it did not seem strange at all, and nobody questioned it.

The church for us had many faces. Pius xII, the Pope, hung on the wall in the kitchen close to the Sacred Heart. The photograph was solemn, antiseptic, and very pious. But it fitted perfectly our image of the Pope. He was a figure situated somewhere between this world and the next, with a direct line to God, and due a degree of reverence second only to the Almighty. Above the little red lamp hung the picture of the Sacred Heart. The eyes in the picture seemed to follow you around, knowing all your secret and most shameful thoughts, and passing judgement. The God that we believed in then was a distant and awesome person. The reality of hell was presented clearly and with graphic imagery even in our young days, particularly in the missions which we had regularly every few years. There was a strong element of fear.

A major factor in experiencing the face of the church was the local priests. The curates of my youth were, by and large, fairly benign men. They were quiet and retiring. They taught us the rituals of serving Mass, and came to check on our religious education in the local school. But they did not leave a great impression on me, generating neither great fear nor much human warmth. But then, living as they did in an old and dilapidated house at the end of an avenue, either alone or with an old housekeeper, their lives did not contain much in the line of human warmth that we could see. The parish priest was of a different mould. He was remote, severe, and very powerful. He did not mix with the people, and we only approached him when it was absolutely necessary, and then with a certain degree of trepidation. His housekeeper was reputed to be almost as forbidding as himself, so that a visit to the parish priest's house could be quite an ordeal.

The Punch and Judy showman came to our little country school one day when I was about eight or nine years old. He was made welcome by the principal teacher, a man in his thirties, who was a very good teacher whom we all held in high regard. All the pupils were gathered into one classroom, the blinds were drawn, and the show began. I can still remember the fascination of it. In the pre-television days, for simple country children, this was a gateway into a world of magic. We alternately laughed and cried as we followed closely the antics of the two puppets on the makeshift stage. We were riveted. But then the door burst open, and the parish priest stood there. Though he was a small man, his position of authority gave him great stature in our eyes. With one swing of his arm, he overturned the stage, destroying the magic by revealing the showman with his strings. And he ordered him out of the school immediately. Then he turned on the principal, and this was a seminal moment in my youth. This teacher whom we looked up to as a source of great wisdom and authority, became like one of us, a little boy, in face of the severe reprimand of the parish priest. None of us children were in any doubt as to where the real power lay in our community.

Another day, cycling home from school with my sister, his car pulled up and he rolled down the window and called my sister over. Hastily dismounting from her bicycle, she approached the car. 'Do you bless yourself with your left hand?' The voice of authority, strong and abrupt. Speechless, she nodded her head. 'Don't ever let me see you doing it again!' The window rolled up, and the car drove away. I witnessed an immediate and irreversible conversion to right-handed blessing, and my sister vividly remembers the encounter to this day.

But the church was also mystery and poetry for us. The gathering of the people for Sunday Mass, and maybe even more significantly, for evening devotions and missions: the singing of the old hymns; the ringing of the bell to announce the presence of the Divine, and the hush that descended on all of us; the candles, flowers and incense. All of these were openings to a world beyond. Even for those of us who lived through it, it is hard for us now to conceive of how central a role the church played in our lives in those days, and how substantially it influenced our way of thinking. Looking back, it seems to have been very oppressive. But I don't think we experienced it as that at the time. It all fitted so neatly into our way of life, and our thinking, that it appeared quite normal. Were we unhappy? Probably not, any more than any generation of young people are unhappy. It would seem to me that we were generally more content than today's youth, because, in a world where advertising was still in its infancy, we had far less expectations, and were more easily satisfied.

But fear was a reality in our lives; fear, inspired by the religious teaching of sin and it's consequences, hell and eternal punishment. One of the nightmares of my youth was the predictions that were made for the year 1960. Some years prior to it, when I was about ten, our weekly Catholic paper carried a prediction of frightening happenings for that year, when God's retribution was going to be visited on the world. There were going to be three dark days, and the state of everyone's soul would be revealed. Those who were of blameless life would shine out, and would spend the three days in prayer. The others, and I knew that would include me, would be shown up for the bad people that we were, and would be forcibly and dramatically consigned to hell. It was a terrifying prospect for a young child. This was published, with front page headlines, in the Catholic paper at the time, which was sold at our church each Sunday, and which we were all exhorted to buy. So it came with official approval, and, in the absence of any comment from the priest about the story, I took it as part of my faith. I suppose my parents, while probably not believing it themselves, didn't feel confident enough in their knowledge of their faith to tell me to ignore it.

These were great years for religious life. Convents, novitiates, seminaries, were bulging. One could say that in many ways the brightest and the best were joining. The candidates on any given year included young men and women of the highest intellectual capability, strong and energetic, and very idealistic, as was common at the time. When I entered the Redemptorist seminary in the middle sixties it had reached an all-time high of one hundred students. There were extraordinarily talented people there. And it was a ferment of intellectual debate and discussion. The two books I found lying on my table in my room, when I first arrived in the seminary after a very strict and enclosed year of novitiate, were Tolstoy's *War and Peace* and Salinger's *Catcher in the Rye*, the great promoter of youthful rebellion of its era. Not only was I encouraged to read them, but the books we were reading were a constant source of discussion among the students. (I understand this was not typical of that time. A contemporary of my own, who was beginning her religious life in a convent, had no such access to literature. She recalls how, tired of reading the *Messenger* and the *Redemptorist Record*, and looking for more intellectual stimulation, she went to her novice mistress with a request for some books, and was curtly told that it would be more in her line to attend to the way in which she articulated the antiphons at the daily recitation of the *Divine Office*.)

It was a very strange and exciting time. The system in which we were living was still largely traditional, and very restrictive. But within it were these hundred young men, carrying on a constant debate on the issues of the day. The fact that many of us were attending the local university made the efforts of the structure to isolate us from the spirit of the times more difficult. Of course it couldn't last, and within a short space of time there began a mass exodus. But by then the Vatican Council, and the general sixties era, had begun to erode the coherent value system on which it was all based. But more about those two movements later.

There were three important factors in bringing so many of us into religious life in those years, and it is hard to measure them in order of importance.

1. As I have said previously, there was a coherence about life then and about what we believed as individuals and as a society, which is markedly absent today. Into this coherent belief system, both the theology and the generally accepted philosophy of the day fitted perfectly. And within all of this, religious life made perfect sense. It wasn't in any sense a contrary statement about the values of the day. Quite the opposite. What were the outstanding features of that belief system?

– That this life was but a brief preparation for an infinitely more important existence, eternal life.

– That in fact this life was not of any great importance in itself except to live it in such a way that you would assure yourself of salvation. And since salvation was attained chiefly by avoiding serious sin, the sinless life was the one to aspire to.

– The great sin at the time, and the one that most endangered your salvation because almost all transgressions were in the serious category, was sexual sin. So the best way of avoiding the dangers in this area seemed to be to have nothing at all to do with sex. The obvious way to do that was to live the celibate life.

– Religious life was seen as a higher state of holiness than any other form of life. It was definitely considered to be in a higher category than marriage, which was somewhat tainted by the impression that it was a legitimised way of life for those who were unable to avoid sexual activity completely.

– Service of others was held up as an important value. You were encouraged to think of others before yourself. And to give your life completely in the service of others was the greatest thing of all. That was what we believed religious life entailed.

– The notion that outside the church there was no salvation. In other words, we believed, and were taught to believe, that everyone who was not a Catholic would go to hell. This included not just atheists, non-believers and pagans, but also believers in the other great religions of the world, and Protestants. There were certain exceptions made to this teaching, in terms of those who were not culpable in their failure to belong to the church, which were clearly efforts to try to soften what was a very harsh doctrine. But it was also a very important and influential doctrine at the time. It had the effect of imbuing us with a sense of zeal, and with the urgency of the task at hand, that of bringing people into the church, which one is more likely to find today in some fundamentalist groups and in some expressions of the Muslim faith. It also effected our view of the third world. The image of the 'Black Babies' was strongly promoted, and we regularly put our pennies in the boxes for the foreign missions. While we were in no sense well off ourselves, we were told by many visiting foreign missionaries that the children of Africa were infinitely poorer than we were. And since service was so strongly emphasised in our upbringing, we genuinely wanted to help them in any way we could. But mostly, they were pagans. And according to our beliefs, when they died they would go to hell. What better way could an idealistic young person spend their life

than to go to Africa as a religious, and convert all these little black
children to Catholicism, so that they would be saved? We were also
encouraged to pray incessantly for the conversion of Russia. Many
of the religious boarding schools of that era observed a period of
silence each evening for that intention. It was, we were assured,
very dear to the heart of Our Lady. I consider that the change in
this belief that there was no salvation outside the church, brought
about partly by the Vatican Council and partly by the inevitable
opening up to the world, was a highly significant change. The difference between believing that your faith is the only correct one and
the only way to God and to attaining eternal happiness, and believing
that there are many different ways to God which should be respected
and cherished, is an enormous difference. Has Catholic theology
ever really explored the implications of this change?

2. Apart from the spiritual gains that went with living the religious
life, there were also more immediate, temporal, rewards. Religious
were highly thought of by people generally, and were given a position of considerable status and influence in society. When I discussed my future with my father that day in the hayfield, I was con-
scious that I was choosing something that merited not just an eternal reward, but also a position in society that would be above that
of most of my contemporaries in the area, whose choice was not
much greater than taking a job in the local Bord na Móna works or
emigration. In those years, when the different levels of society were
fairly rigidly fixed, religious life was by far the easiest way for a person from the lower levels of society to move up the social scale.
Through it one could assume a uniform which was just as respected
as that of the gardaí, or the businessman's suit. There was also the
possibility that one could rise to a position of considerable distinction and authority, like principal of a school or matron of a hospital. These positions would otherwise have been almost unattainable
for a person from the lower classes. For women, religious life certainly gave opportunity to achieve positions of status and authority
that otherwise were not open to them. I am not suggesting that
young people at the time chose religious life in a cynical way in

order to move up the social scale. That was certainly not the case. It is hard to measure how much social factors influenced us, either consciously or unconsciously, in our decision-making, but I suspect they played a bigger part than we realised.

Another substantial temporal reward of religious life was that it gave a person access, not only to secondary education, which was by no means freely available, but also to third level, which in the Ireland of those days was the preserve of the privileged few. We might have had, in our late teens and early twenties, to attend university in full religious garb, with black trilby hats on our heads (mine never fitted properly, and flew into the Corrib one windy day as I cycled over the Salmon Weir bridge, never to be replaced!), but at least we were there getting the benefits of the education, when, in many cases, our parents could not possibly have afforded to send us to university. And amazingly, the ordinary students at the time didn't pass any remarks of the way we were dressed, but accepted us completely as part of the scene. They too were products of the same culture that produced us.

The lure of the foreign missions was an attractive factor. Many of us already had aunts and uncles working in some part of the third world, and we were familiar with their letters and their occasional trips home. Regularly during our schooldays, especially at second level, priests on leave from the missions visited the school and spoke to us. In the context of our limited lives and experience these were often dashing figures. They were great communicators, and they regaled us with stories of their exploits in distant places. In those days travel was very restricted. Most of us had hardly been outside the confines of our own area, except maybe to go to boarding school. The lives these men and women lived seemed so tremendously exciting. Not only were they doing the marvellous work of saving pagan souls for Christ, but there seemed to be great fun and excitement in it too. And travel! How else, in those confined days, was one going to get to see the world? In my schooldays one missioner enthralled us with the story of how the ship in which he was travelling to the missions was hit by a torpedo during the second world war, and his narrow escape. Another, a great story-teller, made India sound like a world of romance and adventure, and fired all our imaginations. All this, and heaven too!

3. A third very important factor in enticing so many of us into religious life was clearly the lack of opportunity at the time. Ireland, before the economic explosion of the Lemass era, was a fairly drab place, offering little enough to its young generations. The big international companies, which now provide so much employment, were largely a thing of the future. Local industry, where it existed, like the Bord na Móna works in my area, was fairly small, and offered neither great wages nor many opportunities for advancement. The lucky ones got called to teacher training, the bank or the civil service. The eldest son inherited the farm. And the bulk of the rest emigrated. Given that limited range of options, what religious life had to offer was quite attractive.

I have overlooked the notion of a call from God in all of the above. We firmly believed that the decision to become a priest or enter religious life was an answer to a direct and individual call from God. A lot has been written and spoken about the nature of this call. Some people said that they experienced some type of dramatic moment of inspiration, similar to St Paul on the road to Damascus. But the general interpretation of this notion of 'call' was that God spoke more quietly and indirectly through the circumstances and events of a person's life, and that a process of discernment was needed to work out the nature of the call. Of course, the times I am writing about were an age of greater innocence, of more simple understanding, than we live in now. Psychology, and the study of the development of the human person, have taught us so much about the complex nature of human motivation, and how easily subconscious needs and desires can masquerade as lofty motives, that we have become more sceptical. What appeared then as an unselfish answer to a call from God to come and serve his people, might be looked on quite differently from today's perspective. We might question now if the decision was made from religious motives at all, or if family, social, economic or cultural reasons had more of a part to play. Kate

O'Brien, writing out of that era, addresses the complexity of a so-called religious vocation in her book, *The Land of Spices*. She writes with remarkable intuition about Helen who became superior general of her congregation. The reality that O'Brien drives home to us is that Helen retreated into a convent because she couldn't accept or even contemplate her father's homosexuality.

Our theology easily accepted the notion of vocation as a call from God and did not look for possible hidden or unconscious motives behind it. So it is easy to see how a minority of sex abusers and paedophiles got through the system. The system at the time, though at one level very strict and severe, was not at all geared to weed out somebody like this. Any type of psychological testing was not introduced until the mid to late sixties, and much later in some places. The numbers were large, so that the individual could easily avoid too much personal scrutiny. But more importantly, the ideal student was considered to be the one who obeyed the rule in all areas, did what he or she was told, and generally kept the head down. Submission to the authority, 'obedience', was the quality most advocated and admired. So it was relatively easy to 'play the game', and get through without too much difficulty.

It would appear to be true that the larger an institution, and the longer and more glorious its lifespan, the more inadequate it is in the face of change. I'm sure that there were some people who recognised that change was coming, but there was a general belief in religious life in those days that things would always remain much as they had been. The enormity of the change that was coming could not have been perceived fully by anybody, but most seemed to have had no inkling of it. That can be seen from the efforts that were made, when things began to fall apart, to continue as if nothing was happening. And that way of thinking and behaving became a feature of one strand in religious life for the next forty years, and sadly, even in the face of the most blinding evidence to the contrary, some people still act today as if nothing had changed.

CHAPTER 2

The old system – before Vatican II

The subject I wish to explore in this chapter is why the traditional system of religious life, which had survived unquestioned for such a long period of time, and which seemed to be at its height in this country in the fifties and early sixties, collapsed so quickly. Why was it so unable to cope with the changes that came about in the world at large? Were there aspects of the system, or of the philosophy and theology on which it was based, that made it vulnerable, or maybe that even made its collapse inevitable?

Forms of religious and community living can be traced back to the very early centuries of the church. In every age there seems to have been people who wished to live some form of dedicated life, and to do it in the company of, and with the support of, others. It has taken many different forms throughout history. The rise and fall of religious congregations has been chronicled by many authors. I particularly refer to the work of Diarmuid Ó'Murchú. The large majority of orders and congregations that were founded at various stages no longer exist. In so far as there is a pattern in history it seems to be as follows:

A man or woman of great faith and leadership ability recognises a need in their particular time and place. They become fired up with the desire to do something about this need. Gradually they gather others around them, who become inspired with the same ideal. In time, this group forms itself into a unit, which in due course becomes a religious community or congregation, taking vows or promises, and living under a rule which is approved by the church authorities. (An interesting point here is the number of founders, for instance Catherine McAuley and Nano Nagle, who did not particularly want to set up an institution, but who were steered in that direction by the church authorities, who needed some way of controlling the development. The church worked on one particular notion of what religious life should be, and to what extent and in how many instances did the setting up of these institutions do violence to the ideas of the founders is hard to assess, but it is a relevant question.)

There are usually substantial initial problems, and some groups disintegrate at an early stage. But if these can be overcome, there is a period of fairly rapid growth and development, in which the zeal of the original founding members is strongly present. The next stage is the period of consolidation. In a sense, one could say that things settle down, both in the good and bad meanings of that phrase. The group expands, makes new foundations, and usually spreads to other countries. Systems of government and structures become solid, and things are running smoothly. Usually numbers continue to increase. The original apostolic need which gave rise to the first coming together of the group is now being tackled on a wide scale, and some new approaches develop. But, as time goes by, dangers begin to emerge. Structures, which were a necessary part of the organisation of the group, can now become solidified. They can become ends in themselves, not yielding to change or adaptation, and instead of being a help they gradually develop into a hindrance. Certain ways of conducting the apostolate, maybe the ways of the founding fathers or mothers, or maybe later adaptations, can become rigid patterns, and people are no longer free to adapt to meet the new needs of a new age. So the very originality and flexibility in the face of a need of a particular time, which started the group off in the first place, has now become impossible. It is discouraged, or even forbidden. Structures and ways of doing things, which were initially put in place as matters of convenience, have now assumed the proportion of household gods. As the Canadian novelist Robertson Davies puts it in his book, *The Rebel Angels*, these household gods can 'sometimes swell to extraordinary size, and even when they are not consciously acknowledged they have great power.' They have become more important than the task in hand. Even ways of dress, which were sensible and pragmatic in the time and place of the original foundation, become rigid and unchanging despite the new requirements of a different place and a different century. And gradually they become a barrier between the congregation and the people they are meant to serve. This goes some way towards explaining why things such as the time of the community morning prayer, or the wearing of the habit, became crucial issues, while people tended to lose sight of the more important matters such as the nature and purpose of religious life itself.

In fairness, it must be stated that none of the patterns I have outlined here are peculiar to religious life. All human institutions have to guard against the danger that the structures, which were set up in order to help a group of people achieve a certain goal, might become more important than the goal. There is always the risk that the main focus of the members subtly changes from trying to do something which was originally inspiring and worthwhile, to preserving the institution to which they belong. In other words, their focus has changed from being outward looking to being inward and self-serving. It is worth noting that while this happens to the institution generally, the individual member is often unaware of what is happening and still believes that he or she is working towards the original goal. The institution evolves structures that re-enforce this belief. Chapters of Religious Congregations, AGM's of Professional Associations, *Ard-Fheiseanna* of political parties espouse the original vision, and drive home a central message – this institution is true to the ideals of the founder.

History tells us that where religious congregations developed in this way, becoming inward looking and self-serving, they gradually began to decay, and slowly died out. Often, of course, the original need for which they came into existence was no longer as pressing, or maybe had been taken on and was being dealt with by organs of the state. So their *raison d'être* no longer existed. The average lifespan of religious orders in the history of the church is around two hundred and fifty years. There have been a number of very significant exceptions to this. These were the ones who somehow retained the flexibility to adapt and change, and to reform themselves to meet new needs in new times, or those whose purpose was of a more global nature, such as praying for the world. This, in my opinion, explains the fact that contemplative congregations are not declining, or at least not declining as rapidly and irreversibly as active congregations.

When we apply this model of foundation, growth, consolidation, decline, to religious life in Ireland, we can chart its course from the eighteenth to the mid to late twentieth centuries. In the era that I am describing, the Ireland of the middle years of this century, many religious orders and congregations were at a clearly defined stage in the process. The eighteenth and nineteenth centuries were a time when a great number of religious communities of a particular kind were formed, the type we call apostolic religious. That is, groups of men or women who lived religious life in community, but whose focus was on a particular apostolate. The great teaching orders of brothers and sisters are good examples of this. They had flourished and grown enormously through the eighteenth and nineteenth centuries. By the beginning of this century, they had reached the stage of late consolidation, where structures and patterns of life, and methods of conducting their apostolate, had become rigidly fixed, to the extent of almost being ends in themselves. This made them peculiarly unsuited to deal with the sort of whirlwind of change that was coming their way. In short, they contained within themselves the seeds of their own decay. What were those seeds?

1. The fundamental one, and the one on which all the others was based, was the nature of the spirituality prevalent in the church at the time, and of course the theology dictated the spirituality. Since religious life is in a sense a microcosm of the church, the defects of this spirituality tended to show themselves more clearly and more quickly there. It was a negative spirituality. It had negative things to say about life, about the world, about creation, about humanity and about the individual. It set up a conflict between the world and the spirit, between the body and the soul. It despised creation. It

proclaimed that life here on earth was not important in itself, but merely a preparation for eternity. It led to the suppression of the human person, who was most of all a sinner. 'Pray for us sinners'; 'Lord, be merciful to me a sinner'; 'Behold me a miserable sinner.' It is not that these sentences are not correct. In fact they state a very important Christian theme. But it was the emphasis put on them that created the imbalance. The system and the spirituality fed into each other. In other words, the spirituality supported the dominant culture of control. This, I believe, was the basic problem, and the other seeds of decay that I enumerate resulted from it.

2. The culture of control resulted in obedience becoming the primary and most important virtue. It must surely be the greatest sign that an institution is too concerned with self-preservation when it places such great emphasis on obedience. I am not suggesting that it is not an important virtue. Some of the great saints of the church have achieved their sanctity by living out this virtue to the letter. But surely the history of religion shows clearly that something which works very well in the context of a particular very saintly life, can become oppressive when applied in a legalistic way to the more general mass of humankind. Obedience, like all virtues, when it becomes too inflated, changes its character and becomes a vice. It needs to be balanced by other virtues, in this case the virtue of freedom for individuals to develop their full potential. The will of the superior became equated with the will of God, and his command was considered the voice of God for the subject. The sound of the bell, ringing for each of the daily exercises, was also considered to be the voice of God, calling each person to the performance of their duty. This did very little justice to the whole mystery and unpredictability of God, and as such was bad theology. But even more, it left itself open to abuse. Elevating any human authority to the level of the divine is very dangerous. It takes great maturity for a person, invested with that sort of power, not to abuse it. I have often wondered if the obvious difficulty the Catholic Church has found with the notion of the individual conscience might not have its roots in this type of traditional attitude. We were told that yes, a person's

conscience is the ultimate arbiter. But that conscience needs to be informed. And one must inform it by finding out and obeying the teaching of the church. The classic catch-22 situation! The underlying message was that the only properly informed conscience was one that agreed with the church. We are gradually becoming more at home with the notion of individual conscience, but the struggle still continues.

3. The notion of uniformity had become a way of life. The training at the time was geared towards suppressing the individuality of the members, and developing people with similar ways of thinking and behaving. Whenever religious of that era begin to reminisce on their novitiate days they tell stories, which can be seen either as funny or horrific, of being asked to do things that were utterly illogical, one of the classics being the possibly apocryphal story of being asked to sow cabbage plants upside down! This was in an effort to teach them to suppress all their faculties, even their intelligence, to the will of the superior. There is no doubt that many people were permanently damaged, or even destroyed, by this type of treatment. In an effort to mould themselves into obedient subjects, they suppressed their own personality to such an extent that they became little more than automatons, with terrible consequences in later life.

4. The system deprived people of any real say over their own lives. Everything was decided for them. Even the most minute details of their lives were monitored and controlled. Each day was laid out according to a strict timetable to be followed rigidly, and any deviation from this needed the consent of the superior. Any form of personal initiative or decision-making was impossible. For example, some Irish sisters in the United States used to wear black habits in the winter and white habits in summer, because the white was more bearable in the heat. The day for changing from one colour habit to the other was laid down, and the whole community changed together, irrespective of the climatic conditions or the needs of the individual. Adult men and women were treated like children. As a result, members tended to remain at a fairly immature and underdeveloped

state, and this made them less effective in the exercise of their
apostolate.

5. Authority was structured and exercised in such a way that the
power invested in the people who were in charge was nothing short
of dictatorial. Luckily, the majority of them were benign in the exercise of that authority, but certainly not all were. All congregations
contain in their folklore many colourful stories of the way in which
particular people ruled with an iron hand, and terrorised the lives
of their subjects. In some congregations the superiors were chosen
rather than elected, so that the individual member had little or no
say over who would be in charge. While there was usually a limit
put to the length of time a person could spend in any particular office, in some instances the power got into the hands of a clique, and
they, through a system of 'musical chairs', kept it among themselves, and the large majority were shut out. This pattern also existed
in congregations whose members had in theory power to elect their
superior. The sociologist, Thomas Bottomore, in his book, *Elites in
Society*, recognises that elites always develop, but it is the closed elite
that is dangerous, i.e. the one that does not allow others in, or only
allows them in on condition that they accept the elite's way of
doing things. This inevitably created a sense of alienation among
some, which was very detrimental to the overall morale of the
group.

6. Religious life is at its best when it is 'counter culture'. It is meant
to stand out in contrast to the accepted values of its day, and to proclaim not so much a different way of living as a radically different
philosophy of life. That is at the heart of the foundation story of
practically all communities. The danger that arises during the consolidation period of any community is that it gradually loses this
quality of 'counter culture' and begins to fit more comfortably into
the value system of the day. While, in some ways, the lifestyle of religious in this time seemed very different to that of ordinary people,
they had in very significant ways begun to adopt many of the values
of 'the world', as it was called in the spiritual books of the time. I
think the most significant and damaging aspect of this was the fact

that class distinction had become an accepted part of the way religious lived their lives. Within monasteries and convents there were, too, different classes of people. I refer to the existence of the priest/lay brother divide in male communities, or the choir sister/lay sister divide in convents. The lay brother or lay sister were servants, and were treated as such. Usually they did not have a sufficient standard of education when they entered to enable them to undergo training for the apostolate, and they were not given any opportunities of bettering themselves within the institute in the form of adult education or skills training. Instead they were slotted into the role of servant, doing all the menial tasks around the house, and looking after the needs of the priests or choir sisters. A lot of the customs were borrowed from the way in which the aristocracy related to their servants. For instance, the brothers had to light the fire in the rooms of the fathers, and collect the shoes that would be left outside the door at night, polish them and return them shining for the morning. There was also quite a strict segregation between the two groups, even though they lived in the same house. At the weekly Chapter of Faults, when the brothers had first confessed their faults, the superior announced: 'The brothers may now leave', before the priests made their public confessions. It was felt better that they would not mix much with each other. A whole theology and spirituality was developed around this lay brother/lay sister lifestyle, and was inculcated constantly at retreats and conferences by the retreat masters, who of course were always priests and consequently of the other 'class'. This emphasised the value of prayer, of quiet service, of submission, the 'apostle at home' as it was called. There is no doubt that some fitted well into this, and lived beautiful lives of great sanctity and service, but when the changes came and people were free to express themselves, it became obvious that many lay brothers and lay sisters were deeply hurt and embittered by the way they had been treated, and carried deep resentments for the rest of their lives.

In this century, I think it is true that this 'class consciousness' began increasingly to influence the apostolate of many religious commu-

nities. For instance, the great teaching orders of male and female religious which flourished at this time had all been founded to educate
the poor. While at primary level they continued to be involved with
all levels of society, and their schools were open to the poorest of
the poor, a change began to take place at second level, where com-
petition was at its keenest. Many congregations provided education
at a nominal cost to the middle and lower middle classes, but increasingly the poor began to go to the small state education sector,
the vocational schools. In many Irish towns and cities a situation
developed where a fairly shameless creaming off was done to ensure
that the best and brightest students went to the religious-run
schools, leaving the intellectually weak, even the remedial, and
those from the disadvantaged part of the town, to go to the vocational school. There also existed the elite schools, both male and female, for the education of the children of the wealthy. These were
run by a few high-profile religious communities. They made no secret
of the fact that they were only interested in the upper levels of
society, and even those few students from lower down the scale who
managed to get in through one or other scholarship scheme were
generally made to feel that they did not really belong: 'Would the
scholarship girls please stand up'! You might have brains, but you
haven't got the class that comes from inherited wealth!

Because they educated the children of the ruling classes, these religious orders carried a great deal of influence at the time, particularly
in the context of an Ireland that was so much controlled by the
church. It is a debatable point as to whether or not religious life can
retain its sense of being 'counter culture' when it becomes such a
close and comfortable bedfellow of the ruling class in a society. I do
not think it is possible, and consequently I would regard the existence
of an upper class group within religious life in Ireland at the time to
be one of the significant 'seeds of decay'.

7. What was known as 'community life' was considered of great importance in the religious living of this era. The members lived together, sharing everything in common. No one kept anything for
themselves; everything belonged to the community. At least this

was the theory, and in most cases it was the reality also. As in all
other areas, this aspect of life was governed by detailed legislation.

While silence was observed for some periods of each day, there were
also times set aside for the members to be together, and to 'recre-
ate'. For most of us who lived through this era the memory of this
'recreation' is not very pleasant. While we spent time together and
talked to each other, there was little enough real communication.
In fact real communication was not encouraged. There was a law
against what were called 'particular friendships'. You were meant to
have the same type of relationship with all members of the community, and not be especially close to anyone. I'm sure this had at least
something to do with the fear of homosexual or lesbian relationships. But it was deeper than that. You were trained to 'forget yourself'. Personal needs were not greatly considered, if at all. The community, the apostolate, and your life of prayer and relationship
with Christ, were all that you could possibly need. If you were not
happy it was a sign that you were falling down in one or all of these
areas. In fact, in male communities there was a type of macho or
hard man attitude. Displays of personal emotion were generally
considered signs of weakness. As a consequence of all of this,
though the members spent a lot of time in each other's company,
there was little enough real human relating. Inevitably there was a
great deal of loneliness and low self-esteem. It is true that you can
live in a house with thirty or forty other people with whom you are
sharing your life, and still feel lonely and isolated. So, when the
changes eventually began to come, the abandoning of compulsory
recreation was a great relief for many.

8. Scrupulosity was a substantial problem in the church in general
in those times, and also in religious life. There were a good number
of people who were mental and emotional wrecks. Hearing confessions of religious could be a painful exercise because of this. Much
of the scrupulousness centred around sex and the living of the celibate life. Religious men in particular were prone to this. Many a
poor priest or brother's life was dominated by worry over their
struggle with 'bad thoughts' or masturbation. People could not de-

velop as full human beings because they were not allowed even to think about their own sexuality, not to mention learning to accept it and integrate it into their personality. This led to a form of religious life that caused the diminution of the human person rather than his or her expansion. How could a person be at home in their own body when they had deep feelings of guilt about their sexual nature?

The other area where it showed itself was in the observance of poverty. The interpretation and observance of the vow of poverty in those days deserves a study all its own. It was governed by rules and regulations even down to the most minute details. Every item of possession had to have the permission of the superior. Even the smallest things, like soap or toothpaste, were covered by the weekly request for permission *'pro rebus minutis'* – for the small things. Each retreat contained a conference on the subject. We were given as example people who left small items outside the door of their room at night in case they would violate poverty by keeping it in their possession, and we were told that we should emulate them. It was a ready-made endless field of worry for the person with a tendency to scruples.

Religious did live simply in those days. Life in monasteries and convents was quite spartan, and they spent very little money on themselves. Generally they didn't have access to it anyway. But the bigger questions of poverty, like the structuring of society and the place the religious occupied within that structure, were never addressed.

9. Of course there was a theology, highly developed and with a long tradition behind it, to back up this way of life. It had an answer and a context for every aspect of the life. This was not a great era in the history of theology. A stagnation had set in after the Council of Trent, and little new thinking had gone on in the previous two centuries. But the undercurrents which led to the Vatican Council were beginning to have an influence. Those among religious who were priests had the opportunity to spend some years in serious

study of theology, and with all its faults it gave them some type of an intellectual basis for their lives. A number of orders put great emphasis on education and intellectual knowledge. But I think that the communities of religious brothers, and maybe even more so, of religious sisters, have a legitimate grievance, in that they were excluded from the study of theology. For many there were only two sources of knowledge in this area, the reading of spiritual books, which was encouraged, and conferences given by priests at retreats. There were two lengthy retreats each year, and also one day each month. The spiritual reading that was recommended at the time was almost uniformly of very poor quality, with the emphasis on piosity rather than on anything of an intellectually challenging nature. Very unrealistic and badly written lives of the saints, making them into almost inhuman figures, and extremely pious books on prayer and religious living, were the usual diet. Often the retreat conferences were no better. Little effort was made to develop the intellectual life. I think it is fair to say that this was a deliberate policy. People who had not learned to think for themselves were much more easy to control, and more inclined to do what they were told, so that they fitted more easily into the system. In general, simplicity was valued more highly than knowledge. The difficulty here was that when things began to fall apart, and they did very quickly, those whose understanding of their life was founded on piosity rather than hard knowledge were left floundering. When they were suddenly opened up to contact with a rapidly changing and complex world, they were left not only without answers but with no resources or developed ways of thinking which could help them to find the answers. Consequently many religious of this century became unhappy and disillusioned in their later lives. They had placed too much faith in the institution which governed their lives, and forgot that it was merely 'an earthly city'.

CHAPTER 3

The impact of the Vatican Council

'Ours is a new age of history with critical and swift upheavals spreading gradually to all corners of the earth.'

This quotation from one of the more significant of the documents to come out of the Second Vatican Council, the *Pastoral Constitution on the Church in the Modern World*, shows that the bishops gathered for the council were aware that there were changing times ahead. But they could not possibly have known the extent of the upheavals that were to come, both in society in general and more especially in the church.

Re-reading the documents of the Vatican Council thirty years later is an interesting exercise. The first impression one gets is how much has changed in the last thirty years. The language would be very different if they were written today, and I am not just referring to the constant use of the word 'man'. There is a great confidence in the tone that is used, as of a body speaking out of an immense conviction about its message and its place in the world at large. That is very striking. I wonder if the church was gathered in council today would it have the same confidence to speak to all humankind with such utter conviction about its relevance to everyone, even the non-believer?

It is also very obvious that the documents came from a gathering in which there was a great struggle being waged between those with different outlooks and perspectives on change. This divergence of opinion shows itself both in the language and the content. In the various documents, and sometimes even within the same document, contradictory opinions are expressed. For instance, in

Perfectae Caritatis, the document on the renewal of religious life, very contrasting sentences can be found.

> 'The up-to-date renewal of the religious life comprises both a constant return to the sources of the whole of the Christian life and to the primitive inspiration of the institutes, and their adaptation to the changed conditions of our time.'

This sentence had the potential for initiating change. But elsewhere in the same document we read:

> 'Religious should be humbly submissive to their superiors,' and 'They should practice mortification and custody of the senses.'

The language and the content of these sentences uphold the very structures that the previous sentence was threatening to undermine.

Perfectae Caritatis is not one of the more significant documents of the council, and in general its tone is quite traditional, but yet it had enough in it to give impetus and approval to a major drive towards change. The need for renewal in religious life is stated clearly, and two principles are laid down: The first one is the importance of returning to the sources, both in terms of the faith and of the particular institute, and the second principle is adapting to the needs of the time.

> 'The manner of life, of prayer and of work should be in harmony with the present-day physical and psychological condition of the members. It should also be in harmony with the needs of the apostolate... with the requirements of culture and with social and economic circumstances.'

The document declared that modes of government should be examined and revised, and it gave a blessing to 'prudent experimentation', and even to 'diversity'.

But I suspect that the real influence of the council on religious life was not brought about by the dictates of *Perfectae Caritatis*, but by other aspects of the event.

Firstly, the fact that Vatican II happened at all was immensely significant. Even if it had never produced a document, its very happening was bound to have great repercussions. To have the bishops and leaders of the church gathered for three years of intense dialogue and discussion about all aspects of the faith changed the whole atmosphere. We had grown accustomed to a church that was dogmatic, provided answers and pre-empted discussion. Now we were witnessing a church that questioned, discussed, and gave permission to people to think for themselves and find new answers, even a variety of different answers. The old notion of keeping your head down, and doing and believing what you were told, was gone. Dialogue had been officially recognised as a good thing. As a consequence, the traditional superior, whose only way of governing was by laying down the law, was suddenly faced with demands for dialogue from his or her subjects. The superiors were in no way trained for dialogue, so that even if they wanted to attempt it, they didn't always know how to go about it. They began to feel very threatened and, as is natural is such a situation, closed ranks and tried to assert more vehemently the old ways. But, devoid of a rationale for imposing their will on others, many of their subjects ignored them and began to go their own way. The breakdown of authority was imminent.

Secondly, the tone of the council, as seen in some of the documents, was extremely important. I'm thinking particularly of the *Pastoral Constitution on the Church in the Modern World.* The church had for so long been almost ghetto-like in its mentality and it was startling to see it suddenly come out and address the whole world, and do so in an open, confident voice. It is the openness that was the most striking aspect: 'We must be aware of and understand the aspirations, the yearning, and the often dramatic features of the world in which we live.' 'Our eagerness for dialogue, conducted with appropriate discretion and leading to truth by way of love alone, excludes nobody ... 'The impact of this on the imagination of religious is now hard to assess, but at the time it was immense. Suddenly, the world was our oyster. Closed doors, high walls, enclosures, were to be tolerated no longer. Why shut out this world with which we were called to enter into dialogue? How can we come to know it, to understand its yearnings and aspirations, if we are locked away from it. This was a dramatic change. 'The world' in religious life terms had been a derogatory phrase, conjuring up sinfulness and evil to be avoided as a serious danger to salvation, and from which the cloister walls and the structured enclosed life protected us. Now it became the place where the action was happening, where the religious must engage, and bring with them the message of salvation to a people hungry for meaning. It was an image to fire the imagination of any young person.

The document also spoke of the importance of the intellect, and of developing intellectual knowledge. 'The intellectual nature of man finds its perfection in wisdom... Our age, more than any of the past, needs such wisdom if all that man discovers is to be ennobled through human effort. Indeed the future of the world is in danger unless provision is made for men of greater wisdom.'

And most of all, it praised freedom. 'It is, however, only in freedom that man can turn himself towards what is good. The people of our time prize freedom very highly and strive eagerly for it. In this they are right.'

I believe it is hard for us today to appreciate the significance of sentences like these, and the impact they made on traditional religious life. Thinking, use of the intellect, having freedom, taking personal responsibility, were now being encouraged, indeed lauded. It is not too strong to say that in a sense they cut the ground from under the form of religious life outlined in chapter two. They destroyed the underlying philosophy and spirituality on which it was based. Unless religious life had the ability to change radically, and to adapt its structures to a very new reality, it could not survive. But, as I've already outlined, religious life in that era was particularly unsuited to the challenge to change and adapt. It was rigid and inflexible – it had solidified.

What was this underlying philosophy of traditional religious life which the council challenged?

1. The notion that religious life was a specially privileged life, with a surer guarantee of salvation. This had been central to the success of the old days. It was a nice feeling to know that your way of life was special, and to believe that it was a more spiritual life than any other. That gave a person motivation to endure the deprivations of the life. But now the council talked about the dignity of all people and all walks of life, and how 'all Christians, in any state or walk of life, are called to the fullness of Christian life and to the perfection of love…' If one could achieve holiness in any walk of life, why then give up so much to enter religious life?

2. The documents had long passages on the dignity and beauty of married love. Gone were the days when marriage was seen as a necessary evil in order to propagate the human species, and as a concession for those who were not able to live the celibate life, which was generally regarded as a much higher state. Now the council declared that marriage was a holy state. And even sex lost its aura of sinfulness: 'Married love is uniquely expressed and perfected by the exercise of the acts proper to marriage. Hence the acts in marriage by which the intimate and chaste union of the spouses takes place are noble and honourable.' The language is cumbersome, and even coy by today's standard. But the message is clear. The church has officially declared the sexual act noble and honourable, albeit only in marriage. From this moment on, celibacy was going to be more difficult. It was easier to convince yourself of the worthwhileness of abstaining from something which was generally regarded as an occasion of sin, and a serious danger to salvation, than something which had become noble and honourable. After the council, the theology of marriage and preaching on sexuality changed from being a negative to a positive message. The religious preacher and teacher had to focus on the goodness and beauty of sexuality rather than on its sinfulness and evil. He or she had to think about it in a new way, and such reflection often caused the person themselves to rethink their own notions of celibacy.

3. The old system was based on the notion that in the will of the superior one heard the voice of God. But the council asserted the dignity of each human person, the importance of developing the intellect, and the need for dialogue. From the moment dialogue entered in, the power of the superior rapidly eroded. A new system of authority, based on a community in dialogue, began to be attempted. But of course the majority of the members, who were trained in the old ways where one did what one was told and did not think for oneself, were very unsuited to this new model of exercising authority. This must have been a terribly traumatic time for some older religious. In the system in which they grew up, authority, if it came at all, came with age. As a young religious one kept one's head down and one's mouth shut. And in that way there was a possibility of making progress later. Now this age group were just coming into their kingdom. But as they at last got hold of some bit of authority it slipped through their fingers. With the best will in the world it was going to be very difficult. And inevitably the best will was not always evident.

A change of this magnitude in something carrying such a long tradition cannot be done without causing much hurt and resentment. Many communities and institutes became deeply divided, and the battle lines were drawn. We all remember from those times the painful efforts at trying to conduct community meetings and reach decisions. Many of the younger members, through their second and third level education, were skilled communicators. They could express themselves well, and think quickly on their feet. Believing that the brave new world had arrived, they were fearless, and impatient of the attitudes of the older generation. Radical speeches, often modelled on the style of John F. Kennedy or Martin Luther King, were the order of the day. Liberal quotes from the likes of Karl Rahner ('For an adult human being to have to ask permission to leave the house is totally contrary to human dignity!'), Paulo Freire or Ivan Illich were used to bamboozle the older members. And meanwhile they sat in silence. They had no experience of addressing the community, and everything in their training taught them to be cautious. Even those among them who were used to public speaking, either in preaching or teaching, were trained to follow set texts and patterns of thought. Thinking on their feet was foreign to them. And the cut and thrust of the old style community life, which could often be harsh on the individual, made them afraid to show their hand too much. So they tended to lapse into a fairly sullen and resentful silence, and gathered after the meeting to bemoan and denounce among themselves what the young generation were coming to. For the first time, the generation gap became a significant and very divisive reality in some religious communities. The world of the older religious was collapsing around them.

Some showed great ability to adapt. But many became lost in confusion, and sometimes in bitterness and resentment. Inevitably there were cases of people who lost heart completely, and died well before their time, because of their inability to cope. My memories here are, of course, of male communities. I understand that the dynamic worked quite differently in female communities, with less emphasis on debate and argument, and less apparent conflict. But the issues they were trying to work through were similar.

Gradually religious learned the skills of discussion and communication, and became quite good at dialogue. They developed a fairly refined system of decision-making at community level, and are now far advanced of what we might call the secular branch of the Irish church, the diocesan clerical system, in their ability to discuss an issue and make a good democratic decision. But the battles that were fought in the process left their mark, and some of the wounds took a long time to heal.

4. With so much prominence given to talk about freedom and dialogue, obviously the notion of obedience would never be the same again. Soon people began to assert that obedience was due, not to the superior, but to the community, and to one's conscience. The clarity of command had dissipated. The structures began to break down rapidly. Uniformity could no longer be implemented. It quickly came to be seen as something negative, and contrary to the

dignity of the human person. It was replaced by its opposite, an emphasis on the uniqueness of the individual, and this led to efforts to develop the full potential of each person. When large institutions suffer such a radical about-face in one of their core values, their very foundations are shaken. For instance, the basis on which the traditional system of formation operated was undermined on this one point alone. One of the longest running sagas of the next thirty years of religious life in Ireland would be the efforts to develop a new style of formation suitable to the new way of thinking. How could people be formed so as to enable them to take responsibility for themselves, their prayer life, their living of the vows, and at the same time inculcate in them a concern for the well-being of others – in short, training people to take care of themselves without becoming self-centred? These efforts have been bedevilled both by a steady decline in the numbers entering, and by an equally steady rise in the percentage who leave during formation.

5. In the stage religious life had reached in the middle of this century, as I outlined in the last chapter, peripheral things had assumed great importance. Because obedience was the primary virtue, external observance of the law was the way in which goodness was assessed. The small details of the law were writ large. Following the council, the initial battles were fought over the structures of community living. Things like the daily timetable, the format of community prayer, whether everyone had to attend community meals together, the compulsory nature of community recreation, and probably most of all the issue of the night curfew, became major bones of contention. As the laws began to be flouted, superiors found themselves with less authority to exercise the traditional sanctions. During all these years the debate waged at two levels. Firstly, there was an immense intellectual and theological debate, sparked off by the council, and fuelled by the outpourings of the new theology and scriptural study. This covered every aspect of the human and Christian life. The debate was carried on with a relish brought about by centuries of relative stagnation in the theological field and no freedom of speech. Secondly, within communities,

there was another debate, of considerably less intellectual weight, but by no means less intense, over the small issues of community living. Some people saw issues like what time a religious should be home at night as of major importance. Maybe they were right, because it was on the observance of rules like this that the whole house of cards was built!

6. The challenge of the council to get involved in the world, and to work for equality and justice among all people, was inevitably going to cause difficulties for certain sections of traditional religious life. It directly attacked the two-tier system that existed within many institutes: 'Unless circumstances do really suggest otherwise, it should be the aim to arrive at but one category of sisters in women's institutes.' It was very much in tune with the call to get back to the original sources, to become again the counter cultural symbol that the original founders and foundresses were. But unfortunately religious life had become much too comfortably a part of the social and political system in Ireland. It had bought into the system, and in fact was one of the great bastions that promoted and upheld it. Religious were not in a position to stand back and begin to critique a society in which they had such vested interest. Since then things have changed, and the voice of religious has become one of the more challenging voices in the area of social policy in Ireland. I refer particularly to the statements from the Justice Desk of C.O.R.I., the Conference of Religious in Ireland. An interesting development in recent years has been the stance of C.O.R.I. on educational, health and social issues. While the executive of C.O.R.I., and the spokespersons for the Justice desk, officially speak for all the religious in Ireland, the reality is that some of the things they say in these areas have not permeated through to religious-run schools and hospitals. And that tends to undermine the radical content of their message.

Summing up a subject as complex as this is difficult, and tends to do violence to all the nuances involved. But in general I think it could be said that the old system of religious life did not encourage people to think for themselves. In fact it positively discouraged it.

The great significance of the council was that it set loose a wave of freedom of thought in the church. And, like the genie escaping from the bottle, once it was set loose it was almost impossible to stop it, as the Vatican authorities have learned to their considerable frustration ever since. Freedom of thought, which inevitably led to freedom of action, was anathema to traditional religious life. A system that was dependent on uniformity and obedience could not cope with freedom. It was the most undermining spirit that the council could possibly have released. Something had to give. And the story of the next thirty years of religious life in Ireland is a story of the efforts made to adapt to the bombshell that hit at that time, and all the consequences that came from it. That is why my main assertion in this chapter is that the Vatican Council took the ground from under religious life as it was lived at the time. The very neat and coherent value system within which it flourished was blown asunder.

Of course it wasn't only the Vatican Council that took the ground from under religious life. All of this was happening within the context of a rapidly changing world, and an Ireland that was being rocked by such a force and speed of change as it had never experienced before in its history. The communications revolution had arrived, which had the effect of opening Ireland up to the influence of the world, and especially that of Britain and America. Ideas and values that had flourished in a closed society were now being challenged from all sides, and since even in society at large these ideas and values were based more on obedient acceptance rather than reflective personal commitment, they were very vulnerable to challenge. Not only the ideas and values, but also the people in power, were being challenged. The symbolic importance of having someone as powerful as the then Bishop of Galway, Dr Michael Browne, called a moron by a young student on national television is hard to measure. The clatter of the gods falling off their pedestals could be heard on all sides.

The economic boom arrived in the late sixties. The effect of this was that opportunities were created for the youth of the country. From now on, ambitious talented young people had a great many

options open to them. For a short period of time, until large numbers clogged the system, almost all of the professions were easily ac-
cessible. International travel became easy and cheap, so that the
awful parting involved in emigration greatly lessened. Students
began to go to the US for the summer, where it became possible to
earn substantial amounts of money, and with plenty of spending
money and a great increase in the number of motor cars, student
life became quite affluent.

Revolution was in the air. The young people were very idealistic. The
works of Marx, Mao's *Little Red Book*, Fidel Castro, Che Guevarra,
and the marvellous oratory of Martin Luther King, were firing the
imagination. For the more intellectual, people like Paulo Freire and
Ivan Illich were eagerly read, with their message of a whole new way
of ordering society and the educational system. A new outlet, very
different from that provided by religious life, was now available to
satisfy the idealism of youth. Marches and protests of all sorts became common. And it was no surprise that the Civil Rights movement in the north was largely inspired by the young people.

Sex emerged from under the carpet. Not only was it being spoken
about, but now it became possible to openly display your sexuality.
A very significant development at this time was the discovery of the
contraceptive pill. It now became possible to separate sexual inter-
course from having babies and this allowed women the same sexual
freedom hitherto reserved to the male sex. Whether or not the actual
behaviour of the young in the way they conducted their relationships changed very much, the impression was strongly conveyed
that in this, as in so many other things, a new age had dawned.

Looking back, it can be seen clearly that religious life was being
challenged and undermined from both within and without, from
the teachings of the Second Vatican Council, and the rapidly
changing environment. How would it rise to meet this challenge,
and had it the resources and the flexibility necessary to survive? The
next thirty years would give the answer.

CHAPTER 4

Great expectations

Excitement is the word that most springs to mind to describe the period in religious life that immediately followed the council. It was an exhilarating time. The council had set a spirit loose in the church which was very much in harmony with the spirit of the age, in that it was a time of great hope and idealism, a time when freedom was in the air. It was a good time to be young. There was a widespread belief, which in hindsight seems incredibly naïve, that we could build a new world, a world of peace and harmony. It is the prerogative of youth to be idealistic and hopeful, even if it is naïve. And this generation of young people were given the freedom to express themselves. The older generation had lost confidence, both in secular society and in religious life. They had seen many of the principles by which they lived their lives collapsing around them, and they did not know quite what they believed in any more. The accumulative effects of two world wars, and most especially the gradual discovery of the existence and nature of the death camps in Nazi Germany, were causing many people to ask very fundamental questions about their own beliefs and about humanity in general. The young, as is their wont, were quick to spot this uncertainty in the adult generation, and to exploit it.

The most noticeable post-conciliar change to hit the Irish church initially was the liturgical renewal. It is generally accepted that the Irish took to this more easily and calmly than many other countries. But then, even in the scale of traditional Catholic countries, we were a nation that was particularly submissive to Rome. I think it was other changes, which also came at an early stage, that had a more undermining effect on the confidence of the adult Irish

Catholic. I refer to things like the easing of regulations about the Lenten fast, the Friday abstinence, and the fast from midnight before reception of communion. We are dealing here with the same problem that bedevilled religious life. Peripheral things had been allowed to assume major importance, and consequently people lost the ability to distinguish between what was central and what was not. Observing the fast from midnight before receiving the eucharist had been considered a very important part of Catholic teaching, and we all grew up on stories of how our ancestors had endured great sacrifice in their efforts to obey it. And, of course, it was imposed with the ultimate sanction of mortal sin attached to it, so that on its observance depended one's eternal salvation. Suddenly, with what seemed like little more than a stroke of a pen, it was abolished. If something could be of such crucial importance one day that you ran the risk of being condemned to hell over it, and be gone the next day, what could any longer be considered secure and unchanging?

Irish Catholicism now began to pay the price for an over-rigid emphasis on the observance of law, and even more so for having paid little attention to trying to educate the ordinary people in the faith. If, for the sake of uniformity and control, people had been kept in ignorance, and deprived of an opportunity to understand the core of their faith, and the reasons behind it, it is to be expected that sudden dramatic change could not happen without undermining the simple notions on which the whole thing had been built. People became insecure. They had often been told that the Catholic faith, as distinct from all the others, was unchanging, precisely because it was the truth coming directly from God. God does not change. He is the same forever and ever. So consequently, they were assured, faith in him does not change either. But suddenly, and almost without warning, it seemed to the average Catholic as if so much of the essentials were being swept away. Those of us who were involved in the apostolate in those days were inundated with questions like: 'How can something be a mortal sin today and be gone tomorrow?' And inevitably: 'What is a sin anymore?' Maybe most undermining of all: 'Are we any different from the Protestants now?' That question had a strong emotional content: Didn't our ancestors die rather than take the soup, and here are we selling out on all that made us different and superior to Protestants!

With the abolition of a lot of the detailed laws and regulations, people were more free to make their own decisions. The primacy of conscience, and the obligation to follow that conscience, was part of the council teaching. But this concept was not at all familiar to the ordinary Catholic. Endless hours were spent, both in small groups and one-to-one, trying to help people who had been trained only to obey, to begin to make personal decisions about their own faith and moral life. It was very slow and painful, and still continues to this day, though a lot of progress has been made, ironically helped on greatly by the difficulty many people experienced with the church stand on contraception.

However, some were unable to make the leap from unquestioning adherence to church law to taking responsibility for their moral choices. Consequently there was a widespread loss of confidence, and confidence is an essential ingredient if one is to pass on a belief system to the next generation. They quickly detect its absence. It was at this point that the breakdown in transmitting the faith from one generation to the next began to happen. It also coincided with a period of immense confusion in the teaching of religion in the schools. The council put paid to the penny catechism, which had been the mainstay of traditional catechetics. It took a good number of years before any adequate replacement was developed. In the meantime, catechetics tended to be haphazard, with a lot of aimless discussion, and little enough imparting of the basics of the faith. As a consequence, a whole generation of Irish Catholics grew up with a very inadequate understanding of their religion.

This is a brief summary of some of what was happening in the Irish church in the years after the council. On the surface it seemed that the changes had gone smoothly. Practice was still very high. There was a lot of enthusiasm for the new ways. But now, with the benefit of hindsight and with dwindling numbers in our churches, we can see that because of the nature of the old-style faith, its unsound foundations had been seriously shaken.

Within religious life, the changes, when they began, were rapid. Very quickly, some of the pillars of the old way of life disappeared. For the younger religious it was a great time. They had freedom. They were full of heady excitement. The windows were open. All the old stale ways were going to be thrown aside. 'Relevance' was the word. The new-style religious life was no longer going to be shut off from the world. Instead it would engage with it, and bring it the message of salvation, not from the remote recesses of monasteries, convents and pulpits, but right there in the heart of the action. 'The world' had changed its hue. It wasn't the source of all evil. It had become the friend which must be understood in order to be redeemed. We donned our anoraks and headed for the pubs with a sense of mission! Thirty years later, those same religious, now much older and wiser, and somewhat battered by the struggle, have learned a lot about the complexity, and indeed the deviousness, of the same 'world'.

The first significant change was in the structuring and exercise of power. New democratic structures were set up at all levels within the system. Power passed from the superior to the community. Decisions that traditionally were made and implemented unilaterally by one person now became the subject of lengthy community meetings. The skills needed for a superior were very different. The old-style dictators were swept away, to be replaced by people who could lead and bring the best out of others rather than impose authority on them. Of course, none of this happened easily or smoothly. If, as I said, it was a great time for younger religious, it must have been an equally difficult time for some of the older ones. For many of them the old way of life had become their security. Both from a personal and a faith point of view, the structures supported them and gave them a sense of safety. Now they saw so much of it swept away so quickly. They were asked to live a new style of life almost devoid of structures, for which they had no preparation or training. To ask an older person, who has lived all their lives in submissive obedience, suddenly to begin to exercise initiative and make personal decisions, is surely a form of cruelty. But some showed a great ability to adapt to change. Even the occasional one who had been a superior in the old ways, and who had ruled with a rod of iron, now took to the new freedoms with relish, and proceeded to enjoy themselves almost as if they were making up for all that they had missed. It must also be acknowledged that there were some who experienced the move towards democracy as very beneficial. Old people, who had lived all their lives in awe of the superior, were not as crippled by fear as they had been. This had to be a good thing.

It would be difficult to overestimate the importance of the daily timetable in the life of the traditional religious. Looking back on it now, it is hard to imagine that we ever lived our lives in such a fashion, but in its day the timetable was a powerful reality. It was known as the *horarium*, and in many institutes it hung at the back of the chapel, emphasising its 'sacred' character. Every moment of a person's day and night was regulated, and governed by a whole series of the most minute laws. The timetable was followed from hour to hour, prayer, study, work, meals, recreation.

In order to leave the monastery or convent, even to go for a walk, the permission of the superior had to be obtained. Even in the silence and privacy of one's room at night there were rules to be observed. A system of zealators meant that each person had someone else whose job it was to observe the person and report any deviations from the rule to the superior. Once a week, at the Chapter of Faults, one had to render an account of one's failures to the superior in the presence of the community, and receive an appropriate penance. These penances always had a large element of public humiliation about them, like having to eat a meal on your knees, or make the sign of the cross with your tongue so many times on a marble slab in the centre of the floor of the dining room at the beginning of dinner, as everyone looked on. Along with being humiliating, this one was dangerously unhygienic! Apart from the apostolic work, which of course was important for preserving the sanity of so many, there were very few outlets from this life. Attending games, going to the theatre or cinema, were all forbidden. Contact with one's family was minimal. Life within the convents and monasteries, though on the surface appearing to be peaceful, was in no sense idyllic. There was far too much pent-up feeling and emotion suppressed within the walls, with no means of escape. Everything was too claustrophobic. Neuroses of all types were not unusual. Many people kept their sanity by bringing common sense to bear on the whole situation and not taking it too seriously. Indeed those who had a sense of humour, and could occasionally stand back and laugh at it all, were the ones who survived best.

Suddenly religious were free. They began to come and go as they choose, merely informing the superior rather than getting permission. It can be no surprise that many religious, both young and old, were unable to handle this freedom, and inevitably mistakes of all sorts were made. The great silence, which descended on monasteries around nine o'clock in the evening, and which imposed absolute silence until after morning prayer, was one of the first casualties. Before long it began to happen that some of the older members, as they made their way to the chapel at an early hour for prayer, were met on the stairs by some of the younger religious returning home from a night of revelry! The shock waves caused to the system by these types of occurrences were seismic. But it also gave rise to a great fund of stories, comprehensible only to those within the system, about the incongruous situations that took place. The deafening sound of an empty whiskey bottle falling slowly and inexorably from one step to another down the main stairs of a monastery, shattering the last vestiges of the great silence, as a group of young religious tried to clear up all the signs of a late night party before the older ones appeared for the new day, is one of the images I carry from those times!

An aspect of this freedom which I feel is significant was that, for the first time, male and female religious could meet and spend time with each other. Going hand in hand with this was a new understanding of the human person, and of each individual's need for some form of intimacy in their lives. The psychology books were telling us that a person who lived a life isolated from human love and affection remained emotionally immature. The traditional way of coping with celibacy, by keeping your distance from the opposite sex, was now frowned upon, and we were told that we needed friendship in our lives. So, convent and monastery parlours became meeting places for young religious, and strong bonds of friendship were developed, which inevitably didn't always stay at the level of friendship.

It was around this time, in the mid to late sixties, that the first major exodus from religious life began to happen. It was the great pride and joy of many Irish parents to have a son or daughter in religious life, but equally it was a source of some considerable disgrace for someone to leave. The term 'spoiled priest' has strong resonance in our tradition. Not only did you bring disgrace on yourself, but on your family as well, if you turned your back on your vocation. It is interesting to note that 'spoiled priest' applied not to someone who has left the priesthood, but to a student who left the seminary. Even to leave at that stage was a disgrace. The notion of leaving after ordination was not even considered. Add to that the factor, which I mentioned in an earlier chapter, of the understanding of vocation that was promulgated at the time. It was seen as a special gift from God, more precious than any other. The fact that it was given to you made you a chosen one, but also with a responsibility to respond. If you turned your back on it, the penalty would be heavy, not only in this life but also in eternity. God would not easily forgive someone who rejected his most special gift. We Redemptorists were told that St Alphonsus, our founder, would be present on the day of judgement to accuse us if we rejected our vocation. So there undoubtedly was for some people a sense of being trapped, both by God and society. I believe that some people stayed in convents and monasteries in the old days who were totally unsuited and very unhappy, but who hadn't the courage to leave because of the disgrace that it would bring on themselves and their family, and the perceived risk to their eternal salvation.

Putting the social and religious sanctions together, it is not surprising that departures from religious life before the council were few and far between. But once the exodus began it quickly became a flood. And so the stigma almost disappeared. Soon there were so many ex-religious and even ex-priests around that nobody took much notice anymore. This was a very important development, and partly because of it the attitude of parents began to change. It was the sixties, and economic opportunities and participation in third level education were greater than ever. There were now so many other options for their children that they had less desire for them to be priests or religious. As so many left, a sense of insecurity developed, and parents didn't want their son or daughter wasting good years trying out a way of life that they would probably eventually leave. As the whole attitude towards sexual relationships became more positive, the notion of a celibate life for their children was no longer as appealing to parents. So their attitude quickly changed from one of strong encouragement, often amounting to a subtle form of pressure, to one of active discouragement. This is surely one reason for the enormous fall in vocations to the religious life in the last thirty years.

When parents became less supportive, or did not support the idea at all, vocations dropped sharply. Society is made up of a number of institutions – religious, economic, educational, cultural and so on. At any given time, one of these can predominate. With the growth of industrialisation and urbanisation in Ireland, the dominance shifted from the religious institution, i.e. the church, to the economic, and the emphasis moved from faith and ideals of service to personal ambition and material success. This is where the faith element comes in. Alongside the economic prosperity there would appear to have been a decline in religious faith. But it could be asked whether it was faith in God that declined, or just faith in the institution of the church?

Another big question raised by these developments is the whole nature of 'vocation'. In what way is it a call from God, and how does he convey this call to his chosen person? How much does environment and upbringing have to do with it? Is it that God called many more people in the first half of the century than he is calling now? Which of the other two possible interpretations might be correct: Did many people join in the past, not because of a call from God, but because of family or societal pressure? Or are there a great number of young people being called by God today who are not answering that call, because we live in what some people might refer to as a faithless, materialistic society? Many of us are still pondering these questions and have not answered them satisfactorily for ourselves.

Other fundamental questions began to be asked. What are the essentials, the core, of religious life? So much emphasis had been put on the externals, on the appearance, that for many people, both inside religious life and outside, these had become the essentials. A religious was someone who dressed in a particular type of clothing, and lived a strict life cut off from ordinary people. What work they did, or whether they worked at all, was secondary. It was presumed that they spent a great deal of time in prayer. Their very existence was what mattered. They were set apart, and became in a sense intermediaries between people and God. The notion of God at the time was one of a severe distant being, pure and undefiled, and not easy to approach. The average Catholic regarded themselves as unworthy to approach and be heard by this God. They needed somebody 'holier' than themselves to speak on their behalf. In an uneducated society this notion of having someone to intervene for you with the people in power was common. Politicians, with their clinics, played the part in secular life. Religious and priests filled that need with God. People came to them with their worries, problems and sins, and asked for their prayers. Because religious were believed to live a particularly pure and good life, God would listen to them.

As long as the religious remained cut off from people, it was easy to preserve this illusion that they were especially holy. But as soon as they began to appear, dressed in ordinary clothes and mixing in the everyday events of society, the illusion was shattered. To see your 'holy man', on whom you depended to mediate with the all-powerful and distant God, sitting in a pub, dressed in a shabby anorak, and drinking a pint, was a test to your faith. Or your 'holy woman', devoid of her veil, and with her hair done, driving along in her car. 'Sure, you have a great time now!' was said so often with a hint of disapproval and even of bewilderment.

Added to this, the theology and preaching about God took a dramatic change. He was brought closer to us, emphasising his warmth, love and mercy. Even the most abject of sinners could approach him and be confident of a welcome. There was no need for an intermediary between God and his people. One of the fundamental roles of religious, that of intermediary between God and people, had ceased both because the religious no longer lived the type of life necessary to fulfil that role, and because people did not any longer feel the same need for such a person. In this, as in so many other areas, something new was called for, a new definition of what was the essential purpose of religious life.

Traditionally, religious had lived a very frugal life. They dressed and dined simply, did not socialise, and travelled very little apart from what was essential for their work. As individuals they had little or no spending money. This was very much part of the understanding of how one should live out the vow of poverty at the time. But also it had to do with the fact that generally the income of convents and monasteries was not very great, and the majority of what came in was ploughed back into the apostolate in which the community was involved. This was particularly true of the great teaching orders, who devoted the bulk of the salaries of their members to the upkeep of the school and the providing of a better quality of education for the student. Around the time that I am describing state support for education, health, and other areas of life was massively increased. In particular the education reforms of Donagh O'Malley meant that in future the State funded 90% of the building and development of schools. It was no longer necessary for the religious to plough so much money back into their apostolates. The state was looking after it. They found themselves with more available money than ever before. And that, coming hand in hand with the new-found freedom, led to more conspicuous consumption by religious. A new lifestyle, more affluent and comfortable, began to develop and became noticeable mostly by the style and variety of clothing being worn by religious, and the number of cars appearing in the carparks of convents and monasteries. The dividing line between religious life and secular life became blurred.

This had an impact on religious congregations in two ways. It added to the decline in vocations. Young people did not see religious life as something distinct, other worldly, different. So why enter it? It also served to lessen the influence of religious. After all, these people no longer appeared different from ordinary Catholics, so why give any special attention to what they had to say on social or moral issues?

All in all, a new and very confusing reality had dawned. Religious life and society were both undergoing a period of great upheaval. Apart from the inevitable conflict within the system, religious increasingly refused to fit into the traditional expectations of society, and began looking around for a new role for themselves. At the same time, society no longer experienced some of the old needs that were behind the expectations, but had new and much more complex problems to face. Could the new-style religious play a part in solving these problems?

The best way to describe what began to happen is in Durkheim's concept of 'anomie'. Increasingly there was a lack of shared values, both in religious life, in society, and in their expectations of each other. When anomie sets in the system that was built around the shared values begins to fall apart, as it must. Morale declines. People become disillusioned as they realise that what they thought would last forever had shaky foundations. They begin to look after themselves, as they care less for the institution. Self-preservation and individualism become the order of the day.

CHAPTER 5

Efforts at renewal

Throughout the twenty years following the council, and indeed to some extent right up to our own time, enormous efforts have been made to try to renew and reshape religious life. An untold amount of time, energy, and indeed money, was spent on these efforts.

There was a marked difference between the response of male and female religious congregations to the situation. The female congregations tried much harder to renew themselves, and were much more willing to give their energy to the task. As a general rule, male religious were more apathetic. They showed reluctance to gather for assemblies and seminars that tried to grapple with the issues. In contrast, the female congregations seemed to be going from one assembly or seminar to another, constantly exploring new ways to live their lives and conduct their apostolates. This difference in response may be linked to the natural differences between men and women. With the coming of the new freedom, men tended to spread their wings and go their own way, and a male dominated society made it easier for them to do that. Few if any radical efforts were made to change the old structures. Instead they were left in place, but largely ignored by the individuals, so that they became almost meaningless instead of being the very powerful forces for control that they had been in the past. This explains the fact that to this day many male religious communities still operate under very similar structures to what were in place forty years ago, but the life-style of many of the members is dramatically different from what it was. Males seem to live more easily with contradiction because their focus is more individualistic than communal. Women made far greater efforts to develop a new form of community living more in tune with their needs and with the age.

One of the more significant efforts in this area was an attempt to develop a new style of organising community based on the notion of co-responsibility and teamwork, rather than the old concept of 'pyramid' leadership, as it was called, meaning one person governing from the top and handing the orders down the line to the different levels of subjects. This was a brave and an interesting attempt. What happened was that in many convents the role of superior was abolished, and the community took responsibility for governing itself. All of the functions of the old superior were shared out, giving each person an area of responsibility, and the larger decisions, both those affecting the individual and the community, were decided by the group as a whole. So, for instance, if the chapel needed redecorating, instead of the superior making the decision and ordering someone to implement it, the community would sit together, discuss if this was necessary, and if they agreed that it was, they would then proceed to discuss the nature of redecorating and the amount of money to be spent on it. As is obvious, it was a slow and cumbersome way of reaching a decision compared to the old way, but the advantage was that when it was decided the community was more likely to support the decision, because they had decided it together, with everyone having an opportunity to have their say.

Those communities who attempted co-responsibility deserve great credit for their imaginative efforts. It was based on the notion of equality and respect for every person, and that all should have an equal say in their own lives.

While these experiments worked well in particular situations and for periods of time, ultimately they were a failure to the extent that they did not succeed in establishing a new structure for organising religious life. There were a number of reasons for this:

1. Like most efforts at experimentation in the Catholic Church, Canon Law and the Roman authorities were a problem. The law stated that each religious community must have an officially recognised superior, and that this authority should be vested in one person. So they refused to give recognition to communities of co-re-

sponsibility. In the best traditions of Catholicism, an attempt was
made to find some way around this, and the solution was to ap-
point an external superior, or leader, as she became known. This
was a sister from another community who would fulfil the requirements of the law by acting as superior of a community while not ac-
tually living in that community. It was an ingenious way around
the law, but it ultimately served to weaken the experiment. These
'leaders' had no clearly defined roles, having been appointed purely
to fulfil the requirements of the law, so there was no predicting how
they would behave in their position. Even in the situations where
they behaved with great sensitivity, their very existence was a nega-
tion of what was being attempted. At present we have in some congregations a situation where one person is acting as external superior
or 'leader' to four or five different communities.

2. The notion of co-responsibility, equality, everyone having a say
in decision-making, is excellent. But as an idea it is directly contrary to the traditional notion of obedience to the will of the superior
as the will of God, which had been central to religious life before
the council. Most of the people who were now being asked to implement this new style of community living had been trained in the
old way. They were mostly in their middle years or older. It was
probably expecting too much of them to be able to adjust to something so new, and something which in itself, with the best will in
the world, would be difficult to implement anyway. Take any group
of human beings and ask them to live together in harmony, exercising co-responsibility in all areas of their lives, and they would find
it difficult. But to ask a group of people who had been trained into
submissive obedience to do so was probably asking too much.

3. Co-responsibility is an inefficient system of government, both in
terms of time and energy. Even small decisions can take a long
time. One or two people, by adopting negative positions, can assume immense power in the group. They can block consensus, and
so create deep feelings of frustration and anger. In a power vacuum
powerful people tend to emerge to fill the vacuum. If they are positive
people they can make a great contribution and draw the best out of

everyone else. But if they are negative and destructive in their attitudes, as is so often the case with people who emerge to fill power vacuums, they can make the experiment unworkable. In order that co-responsibility work well it would be necessary for the group to be very united in its purpose, and inspired by a deep sense of enthusiasm. As I have said elsewhere, in most religious groups that was no longer the case. The original inspiration had been replaced by staleness and decay. What was needed, most of all, was a new vision. Attempting new structures without a new vision was futile. Both the requirements of Canon Law and the general staleness were serious obstacles to any new vision developing.

A feature of this time was the emergence of the expert, or the 'guru' in religious life circles. Women's groups, in particular, felt that they needed to be guided through all these efforts at renewal. Each time they met for a Chapter or an Assembly, they brought along one of these experts to guide them. As is the nature of supply and demand, the more groups looked for people to lead them, the more experts emerged. Initially these were all priests belonging to male religious communities. One of the ironies of the situation was that in many cases the male communities from which these experts came were making fairly inadequate efforts at renewal themselves, while at the same time going out confidently to lecture the women, who were far advanced in their thinking and their willingness to experiment. But women religious had been for too long accustomed to looking to priests for guidance in all situations for them to change easily. In more recent years they have begun to free themselves from this male dominance, and they have produced experts of their own. Indeed some women who themselves have departed religious life are now making a good living out of directing those who have remained.

Another big effort at renewal, again adopted with more enthusiasm by the female than the male orders, was in the area of spirituality. The traditional spirituality of religious life, meaning for the purposes of this work the spirituality of the first half of this century, was quite narrow. There was a great emphasis on doing certain duties each day, saying specific prescribed prayers. Most religious, every day, did the following: they recited the *Divine Office*, mostly together, though sometimes in private, said or attended Mass, said the rosary, made the Way of the Cross and sometimes another similar exercise called the Way of Bethlehem, made a visit to the Blessed Sacrament which consisted of saying specific prayers, and did two or three periods of meditation, each of half an hour duration. The periods of meditation were in the morning and the evening, with sometimes a half hour also in the afternoon. The type of meditation prescribed was of a particular nature, involving active rather than passive or contemplative prayer. It was usually done in common. A short passage was read out, either from the Bible or from some spiritual book, at the beginning of the meditation, and again half way through. The individual was taught to reflect on that passage and pray out of it for the particular period of time. My own experience, and I suspect that of many others, was that this was a fairly arid form of prayer. A lot of the time was spent in trying to cope with 'distractions', which were regarded as such an enemy of prayer at the time. Many a conference was given at retreat time on distractions and how to deal with them. The notion of contemplation, of quiet contemplative prayer, was not encouraged. It tended to be viewed with suspicion as being Eastern in origin, though in fact there is a strong contemplative tradition in Catholicism, coming from great mystics like John of the Cross and Teresa of Avila

This, in summary, was the prayer life of religious. It was big on quantity, with anything up to three or four hours spent in prayer each day. In common with all other aspects of life at the time, there was a strong sense of obligation involved in this prayer. It had to be 'got in'. Most religious went to confession once a week, and a regular sin confessed by them was not getting all their prayers said. Going to confession weekly was not helpful. Obligation was a feature, not just of the prayer life, but of all aspects of the spirituality of the time, so that feelings of guilt were common. The weekly confession, allied to the Chapter of Faults, tended to increase guilt, and often crippled the person emotionally.

The new type of spirituality that began to develop was greatly influenced by Eastern mysticism. Contemplation, the prayer of quiet
stillness, swept through the convents and monasteries, and was
adopted by many with enthusiasm and great relief. Years of struggling
with distractions at morning and evening meditation, and trying to
find some food for thought in the prescribed readings, made people
ready to accept anything that might be new or fresh, and represented
a different way of doing things. Soon, tapes and books by Anthony
de Mello and John Main became the order of the day. For many,
directed retreats replaced the traditional preached retreats, and spiritual directors were acquired to be guides in these new ways of praying. Retreat centres were set up specialising in different aspects of
the new spirituality, and they thrived for a period. The old spiritual
reading books were put into the library to gather dust, and were replaced by an outpouring of new literature on prayer. The charismatic movement was a big influence. Many religious got very involved in it, and rejoiced in its spontaneity and freedom. Again it
was such a relief, after the rigidity of the old ways, to be able to pray
as the Spirit moved one. Indeed the whole theology of the Spirit
began to have an immense impact in terms of freeing people up,
and giving them the courage to explore new ways of prayer. One of
the consequences of all this was that the traditional structure of
prayer broke down, and all that was left in terms of structure was a
remnant, usually involving no more than the common recitation of
morning and evening prayer from the *Divine Office*, and the common celebration of the eucharist, daily in female institutes and in
communities of brothers, but only occasionally among communities of priests, who tended to say their own Mass privately on days
when they were not saying a public Mass.

Efforts were made to replace the old prayer structures by new
forms. The most notable attempt at this was faith-sharing. This
was where a group of religious within community came together to
reflect on their lives in the light of the gospel, and to pray together.
It might seem to the outsider that this should have been a natural
enough thing for religious to be doing, in view of their commit-

ment to Christ and to each other. But in fact it was extremely difficult, and most of the attempts at it did not last very long. I think
one reason why they did not last was that this method of prayer involved too much and too rapid a shift from the old mentality of religious life. In the old system people had learned to be cautious.
There was so much emphasis on outward observance that inevitably people, to some extent, learned to 'play the game', and
keep their own thoughts to themselves. It was a survival technique.
Faith-sharing involved being open about your inner and intimate
thoughts and feelings with other members of the community. The
cut and thrust, and indeed the harshness, of the old system had
taught people not to trust others that much. So they held back. As
one man said, when, after about three sessions of faith-sharing in
his community, it began to get a little personal, and he was asked to
share with the group something about his living of the celibate life:
'Anything I have to say on that matter I will say to my confessor!'
End of sharing.

As well as this, it is important to remember that under the old dis-
pensation religious had often been told that they were worthless. It
was part of the general attempt to keep people down and make
them submissive. Fear often dominated their lives, and attaining
any level of self-esteem was a struggle. As a result, many were afraid
that if they really shared their faith (and its attendant doubts) they
would be unmasked as 'unworthy', 'unholy', and the big sinners
that they had often been told they were. Without the openness necessary for success, efforts at faith sharing usually petered out fairly
quickly.

With the old prayer structures gone, and attempts to create new
ones proving futile, the amount of time that the community spent
together in prayer declined drastically. When it became recognised
that there were many different ways of prayer, and that individuals
had the right to choose their own way, attendance at even the few
remaining formal acts of community prayer was often sparse. Some
religious asserted that they found the common recitation of the
Divine Office boring and empty, and indeed irritating, and stopped

attending. The superior no longer had the power to insist that they attend. In reality, it quickly became the case that some communities seldom if ever came together to pray as a full community. Prayer became increasingly an individual act. As one might expect, in this situation some people prayed a great deal, and others hardly at all. But the effect on community life of the decline in common prayer had to be significant.

The setting up of new forms of community living became another feature of renewal. Now that the whole attitude to 'the world' had changed, and that they no longer believed that they should shut themselves away, many religious became very critical of the large convents and monasteries. How could a person be in touch with people in any real way while living in one of these large institutions? The sheer size of the buildings, often surrounded by high walls, and with steps leading up to a fairly formidable front door, was felt to be a deterrent to the free access of people. Also, living an institutional life, where all your needs are catered for, where meals are put on the table three times a day, and where you are protected from many of the ordinary daily problems of people, was considered by some to be an unsatisfactory way of life. Cushioned from the harsh reality of so many people's lives, the worries about marriage and family, employment and finance, institutional living could become very cosy and self-centred. Now that there was more money available, and less restriction on the use of it, it became possible, if one wished, to live a very comfortable life indeed. The debates on the vow of poverty and what exactly it meant in today's world became intense. Did a life of evangelical poverty involve having a very slim wallet and living in what Eamon de Valera called 'frugal comfort', or had it more to do with a detached attitude of mind towards material things?

In an effort to find new answers to all of these questions, small groups of religious, again mostly women though a few male groups did attempt it, moved out of the large institutions and set up communities in ordinary houses in estates in the towns and cities around the country. Usually there were three, four or five people in these communities, and the normal pattern was to acquire two adjoining houses in an estate, and convert them into one dwelling. Some of these communities were in privately owned middle-class areas, while others moved into large corporation estates in deprived urban settings. There were, and still are, so many of these communities, and they are so varied, that any comment on them will inevitably be general, and will not apply equally to all. In most cases the religious who lived in these small communities were professional people, teachers, social workers, nurses, which meant that they went out to work each day and their contact with the people in the estate was tenuous. Usually one member of the community, maybe an older, semi-retired person, tried to get involved in some way in the area through some form of voluntary work, particularly if the area was poor. In the middle-class areas the religious tended to settle in relatively easily, because their professional lifestyle was similar enough to their neighbours, but the communities in the poorer areas were more problematic. The religious person was normally from a middle-class background, highly educated, working, and driving their own car. (Finding where the religious lived in an estate was never difficult. It was always the house with two or three Toyota Starlets or Ford Fiestas parked outside, or with an extra wing built on.) Their interests and attitudes were understandably very different from the people among whom they lived. While they made great efforts to live simply and to drive small second-hand cars, it was still only the very exceptional person who was able to bridge the considerable gap between themselves and their neighbours.

The people who attempted these experiments deserve great credit. In some cases they involved great upheaval for people at an advanced stage in their lives. There are still a great many of these small communities in existence, and it is probably too soon to make any definite assessment of them. But, allowing for that, I think it is fair to say that the experiment has not as yet given us a new vision of religious life, or created the impetus or energy for new growth. Some of the reasons for this are the following:

1. Most of the people who attempted these experiments were too

set in their ways, and had lived too long in large institutions, to be able for the type of change necessary for this very new style of living. Often it was simply a case of the old ways transplanted into a new setting. People weren't trained sufficiently, or in some cases at all, to cope with the new demands involved in the experiment.

2. Religious life in Ireland has been for a long time solidly middle-class. To expect people from this background to be able to live among the socially deprived and really share their lives was expecting too much – it was unrealistic.

3. Experimentation is often dogged by the simple fact that the people who volunteer for a new project can often be the people who are least suited to implement it. I have the impression that there was a great variation in the seriousness with which superiors of different congregations took these new experiments. Some saw them as very important, and chose the best available people to be a part of them. Others used them as a way of placing difficult members, who were generally unsettled. In cases where this happened the new experiment had no hope at all. If something new is to have any chance of success, there must be a careful screening of personnel. Living in a small community is much more difficult than in a large house with many members. In the small house there is less opportunity for people to escape from each other. As a consequence, some of these communities had great difficulty in getting on together.

A final area that caused substantial problems during this time of change was formation. The old way of life was gone. Religious were not living it any more. A formation system that prepared candidates for a life that was no longer being lived had to be changed. But the problem was what should be put in its place? No new way of living the life had established itself sufficiently to indicate that it might be the way for the future. It was a time of great flux and change.

It was also a time when there was a considerable divergence between theory and reality. All through these years, marvellous documents were emanating from Chapters and Assemblies about how the life should be lived. But one of the big features of this era was how little impact all these documents had on the lives of individuals. It was in some senses a schizophrenic time, as people more and more went their own way, ignoring the mountains of theory emanating from above. This left the people in charge of formation in a very difficult situation. How do you prepare young people to live a certain type of life when there was no clear idea as to how this life would be lived into the future? The pace of change was so dramatic that any form of certainty was hard to establish. Do you build your system around the theory or the reality? In most cases the students were immersed in the new documents with all their idealism, and then became disillusioned, and their directors frustrated, when they quickly learned that the reality was at odds with the theory. All they had to do was look at how the professed members of the congregation lived.

Attempts were made to train formation personnel as fully as possible. They were sent for long courses to Rome, the United States, and elsewhere. But these training centres were faced with exactly the same dilemma, also not knowing clearly what type of training to give. In the absence of a clearer plan, often they simply fell back on training people in spirituality and spiritual direction which, though worthwhile in itself, was not adequate for the complexity of the job they were taking on.

Another factor that militated against a confident formation programme was the spirit of the age, which emphasised personal development. Within this emphasis there was a hazy notion that all that was necessary was to set up the right environment and people would grow and develop into mature human beings. It put great store on listening to a person's feelings. It did not take sufficient account of human nature, of the need for discipline, of the difficulty of doing the same thing day in, day out, regardless of how one felt. Formation directors found it difficult to set up a timetable, or, to use the old word, a *horarium*, for their students or novices, who often had time on their hands which they did not know how (or lacked the discipline) to fill constructively. Vagueness abounded.

Some emerged from this system lacking the personal discipline which is essential in order to keep a shape on our lives.

Vocation directors, as they were known, the people whose responsibility it was to get new recruits for the order, were under pressure too. As numbers of applicants declined, they found it harder to fill the places in the institutes of formation. Inevitably there was a period during which, in order to keep numbers up, they allowed standards to drop. Particularly during the seventies many joined who, for various reasons, were not suitable. Directors of formation found themselves dealing with difficult and disturbed individuals at a time when they were desperately trying to establish some form of stability. As a consequence, while large numbers were still entering during this period, most of them were leaving very quickly. This created immense problems, and led to strict systems of screening being set up to assess applicants. When this happened the numbers fell dramatically, making it difficult to sustain morale among those who remained.

In many ways, the people in charge of formation had the most difficult part to play during this period. Their task was not clearly defined, the material with which they had to work was often of poor quality, and in terms of providing new members to their order or congregation the results were insignificant. Men and women of great dedication and expertise spend years working with groups of young students, only to see almost all of them pack their bags and leave. Today, with only a tiny number entering, things are not getting any easier.

These were some of the efforts made at adaptation and renewal. There were many others, but I have picked out the ones that I regard as being most significant. It has to be acknowledged that there was a lot of courage shown in these experiments. If a judgement is to be made on them in terms of their pointing a way to the future, I believe it has to be said that they have failed. We are no nearer knowing with any certainty how to live the religious life in this society at this particular time. As time passes, the situation becomes more critical.

CHAPTER 6

Turning inwards

It would appear to be the nature of human existence that the pendulum swings from one extreme to the other, and that human beings find it difficult to discover and preserve a balanced middle ground. In Ireland we have emerged out of an era in which the individual was seen very much in the context of the community and society in which he or she lived, and the good of the individual tended to take second place to what was known as the common good. This is typical, and indeed essential for the preservation of any closed and authoritarian society, as I think Ireland could fairly be described in those times. One of the strengths of the form of religious life that was lived at that time was its harmony with the society around it. It too was very authoritarian, and it strongly promoted the value of self-denial, or self-abnegation as the spiritual books called it. This approach to life has, of course, strong roots in Christian teaching and tradition. Christ 'humbled himself and became obedient even unto death'. 'Not my will, but yours be done,' were some of his final words.

The Christian understanding of loving involves a lot of self-denial, and a willingness to put the other person first. I think it is fair to say that traditional religious life was quite happy to put great emphasis on self-denial. It suited the system to do so. In order to smoothly sustain the authoritarian system you needed very compliant people, people who were willing to forego their own opinions and judgements in favour of the common good. This common good was defined by the rule and interpreted by the superior for the community. Consequently the system of training that I have described in an earlier chapter was developed, to produce these submissive and compliant people. For many years it was very successful. One could say that not only was the religious system shaping people to suit itself, but that it also shaped the teaching of the gospel, by emphasising some aspects and ignoring others, all to fit its own needs. I am not suggesting that this was done in a cynical fashion, or that indeed it was particularly unusual. It was simply doing what many institutions, social, political and religious, have done before and since down through the history of the world. It had fallen into the trap of seeing the preservation of the institution as the primary end.

There was bound to be a reaction to this, and when it came it took many forms. Inevitably one of them was an espousal of the concept of personal freedom. Unfortunately, as can so often happen, this sometimes became a mirror image of the old attitude, in that it was espoused as an ultimate value, more important than any other, and used to ride rough-shod over everything. But this was not always the case, and the right to exercise personal freedom is very important to all of us. Gradually, and I suppose taking its cue from what was happening in society at large, the idea of developing oneself to the fullest potential emerged, and was adopted with some considerable enthusiasm as a project by many religious. It was a good project. To make maximum use of the capability that a person possesses is one of the great and life-long tasks which should engage all of us. Like the notion of self-denial, this also has strong roots in the teaching of Christ. He valued every human being, even the poorest and most insignificant, and taught that everyone should have the opportunity to live their lives in freedom and justice. He told us that the Father loved each one with an infinite love. 'Every hair on your head is counted.' Each person as an individual is important and significant in the eyes of God, deserving of respect and dignity.

What could only be described as a big industry rapidly grew up around this new enthusiasm for self-fulfilment. Both in Ireland and elsewhere, courses, seminars and retreats began to be offered on one or another aspect of self-development. Around this time, because of a decline in vocations, many seminaries and novitiates were no longer needed for the purpose for which they were built. Rather than selling them, some were developed into retreat and conference centres. The decision was based not so much on the need for these centres, but on the fact that a building needed to be used, and new ways needed to be found to support it's upkeep. The decline in vocations was still at too early a stage to be able to say with any degree of certainty that these buildings would never again be needed for their original purpose. So, to find another purpose for them in the short term seemed a very sensible thing to do. Consequently many retreat centres were established during these years. The demand for new-style courses was a happy development for them.

People needed to be trained to run these places and to conduct the new style courses. Many religious went to America for one and two year training courses, and came back to work in the centres. If you look through the programme of any retreat or pastoral centre today you will see now this type of course has become so much a part of what they have to offer. (Though maybe in the last two or three years there are indications that it has run its course, in a manner of speaking.) High on the list were the self-discovery techniques known as the Enneagram and the Myers-Briggs programme. Most religious have done one or other or both of these at some time over the last twenty years, and have spent a period of their lives classifying themselves in terms of what number they are on the Enneagram scale. Even those of us who haven't done the course have sat in on conversations in which others, fresh from their weekend experience, have informed us with great certainty which classification we belong to. 'You are a four!' To which some expert other would reply: 'No, he is a five, with a wing in a four!' Like so many modern enthusiasms it had its own terminology, which gave it an air of mystery, exclusiveness and superiority.

Another aspect of this movement, also promoted by the new retreat and conference centres, was a demand for individual spiritual guidance in the form of directed retreats, where a person spent a given number of days in silent retreat, meeting each day with a director, discussing one's spiritual life and being guided in prayer. The spirituality of the old system was communal, in the sense that it was based on common practices and common attitudes. The normal way used to measure the holiness of the person (something which should not be done at all!) was how well they observed the common practices and were obedient to the rule. Any sort of individualism in prayer or practice was viewed with suspicion. This system, while being very desirable for the smooth running of the institution, was not good for the person. In many cases it did violence to the spiritual lives of individuals. Anything we know about God suggests that he relates in a very individual way with each person, and efforts to confine this relationship to common practices and attitudes are bound to do damage to some. Directed retreats were welcomed with relief by many religious, in that they gave them scope to develop their own individual form of spiritual life and prayer. People who for years were bound and confined by forms of prayer and spiritual reading which they had experienced as sterile, suddenly took wing and began to soar into a new realm of spiritual existence.

However, there were negative aspects to the directed retreat. The fact that it (and the thirty-day retreat) are based on Ignatian spirituality has never been highlighted or critically analysed. Also, there was a tendency among some of the devotees of the directed retreat to cast aspersions on other types of retreat. Prayer, having ceased to be a sterile exercise, became, for some, a competitive one. A demand for people who could direct this type of retreat grew, while the traditional conductor of preached retreats found himself facing unemployment. Again, America became the place where many went to train for this work.

I find it hard to assess the worthwhileness of this whole change of attitude. There is no doubt that each aspect of it is good in itself, and that many individuals benefited greatly from the courses. The personal development courses may have enabled individuals to grow, and this was a very necessary corrective to the old days in which the needs of the individual were largely ignored. But it would be hard to overemphasise how much it changed the face of religious life. It ran contrary to one of the traditional bedrocks of the system, the notion of common life and practice, and as such I believe it was a major factor in the disintegration that began to take place. As people got to know themselves better, and to focus on developing their own potential, and without the shared value system and the dynamism of the earlier years, individualism became rampant. People began to go their own way, and the common focus and the unified goals of the community were not strong enough to hold things together.

While self-fulfilment is undoubtedly a good and a necessary thing, it too contains its own pitfalls. There is a danger that it can become a self-indulgent pursuit. Religious life today, because of its transitional nature and lack of vision, does give people the opportunity, if they wish, to lead comfortable, self-serving lives. How much does the presence of this type of person sap the morale of the whole group?

The fact that so many religious went to America for training during these years is probably also significant. It was a natural happening, because it was said that America, and especially the United States, was where the best courses were on offer. But maybe there wasn't enough consideration given to the values that underpin the affluent American lifestyle, or to the content of American-based training programmes. As a society, it tends to be very individualistic and promotes in so many ways the notion of every person for themselves. Did this have an effect on the social consciousness of Irish religious generally? Did it effect the willingness of some to get involved in the rough and tumble of social action and in work with the poor? In asking these questions, I am not suggesting that religious are not involved at this level. Of course many are. But I feel that the possible effects of American training on the social consciousness of Irish religious is worth looking at.

I said above that many of the self-development techniques had their own terminology, which created a sense of exclusivity, a feeling of belonging to a special group or club. This brings me to the problem of language. During the period since the Vatican Council, a form of language has grown up within the broader religious life community which is used widely in documents, books and seminars, but which is to a fair extent incomprehensible to anybody outside of this community. This type of development is not peculiar to religious life. Many other organisations and interest groups develop a specific type of language which they use among themselves. Sometimes, because of the technical nature of the particular subject, this is unavoidable. For instance, people from the computer world speaking among themselves about their profession, are almost impossible to understand by those outside this world because of all the technical words and phrases they use. So much so that the term 'computer-literate' has been coined to describe those who understand it. Other professions, I suspect, develop their language in order to preserve their exclusivity, and keep outsiders at a distance. But for religious to have a specific language of their own, not understood by people outside their exclusive group, is not helpful. People who are professed followers of Christ, and whose purpose, in one form or another, is to preach the gospel, need to be able to communicate easily with the widest possible range of society. But if you read the documents, and many of the books, that have been produced within this circle in recent times, they are often full of a terminology which does not connect with the experience or way of speaking of people in general. What type of language am I talking about? Let me illustrate, exaggerating a little for effect. In religious life we don't do an ordinary job of work anymore. Instead we 'gather' in a 'cluster' to 'initiate' a 'process' of 'sharing', to 'discern' what 'ministry' we are 'called' to on our 'journey'. We look to our 'leadership team' to 'facilitate', 'animate' and 'energise' us in 'owning' our 'stewardship'. In this we are 'making a statement', while 'affirming' and 'articulating the pain' of one another. When the 'process' is completed, we 'celebrate'.

I believe that the development of this type of language, which is no longer just a religious life problem, but has become more widespread within the whole church, has been one of the real tragedies of the church in our time, and has done a great deal to limit its effectiveness. I think it is one of the reasons why people find much of what passes for preaching in our churches today so vague and unconvincing and generally unsatisfactory, like being 'beaten to death with cotton wool' as one person so colourfully described it. I come from a Redemptorist tradition, and while our traditional style of preaching has been widely pilloried for its supposed 'hellfire and brimstone' content, it contained strength and style both in it's language and in it's delivery. I often recall the opening sentence of the traditional sermon for the first night of a mission. The preacher, dressed in full regalia, with a large crucifix hanging at his chest and a biretta on his head (both marvellously effective in terms of visual communication) mounted the pulpit and began with a quotation from scripture:

'It is appointed unto man but once to die, and after death the Judgement'.

Then he blessed himself, placed the biretta on his head with a dramatic gesture, allowed the silence to continue for a moment, and, when he had total attention, proclaimed:

'My dear brethren, as I gaze down tonight at your upturned faces, I know not your names or your ages; of your station in life I am also ignorant; I know not if you be rich or poor, strong or weak. But there is one great truth I know about each and every one of you, one great eternal truth: That each and every one of you will one day die!'

We can see how it put the fear of God into people! I am not suggesting for a moment that was the right thing to do, or that we should revert to that way of preaching today. The content is of its day, and would not communicate to a modern audience. It was militaristic, authoritarian, and of course very much a male language both in the concepts and the type of words used, as also in the delivery. But note the colour, and yet the simplicity, of the language, and the strength and clarity of the message. It was powerful communication. No wonder we meet so many people around the country who still remember the old-time sermons.

If I can be permitted to parody a little, the more extreme style of modern preacher might put the same message something like this:

'My friends, it is indeed a great privilege for me to be with you tonight, so that we can share these precious moments together. I haven't as yet got to know you by name, but I can sense the warmth of your welcome, and I already feel completely at home among you. A special word of welcome to those of you who feel broken in spirit, fragile, those of you who are vulnerable. You are especially dear to my heart. All of us tonight have one thing in common. All of us share in the great mystery of life, and will one day have to cross that threshold that leads from this world to eternity, where we will be secure in the arms of our loving Father.'

Language is so important. It is our main vehicle of communication. And yet, at its best, it is an inadequate vehicle. I have parodied above some of the ways religious use language today. It would be equally easy to parody the traditional religious language – 'Transubstantiation', 'Almighty', 'Eternal', 'Omnipotent' one could go on. How effective were words like these in communicating the faith to the people? Maybe it is that we have just replaced one form of jargon with another. It has got to be said that we are living in a transition time, and transitional language cannot have the clarity and directness of the language of a settled era. We have also become much more aware of the need for inclusiveness in our use of language. So to some extent it is inevitable that today's language will appear softer, less certain, than the language of the past. The question I am struggling with here is whether the religious language we are using today is the necessary type of language for a transition time, or is it, even to some extent, a language developed to create exclusivity and protect ourselves from the realities of our own situation and of the world around us?

Where did the new language that I am talking about come from? There were many influences, but I will mention a few which I feel were important.

First, there was the charismatic movement. This movement has had many and varied expressions in different parts of the country over the years, so it is hard to categorise, and I don't wish to be in any way dismissive of it, or fail to acknowledge the good it has done. Many people have been greatly helped through charismatic prayer groups, developing a deep relationship with God, and being challenged in their Christian commitment. (Here I find myself using the new language – 'challenge'; 'commitment'! It is so pervasive it is hard to escape! What I should be saying is that because of involvement in the charismatic movement people took their faith more seriously.) It has helped others to face extremely difficult situations in their lives and come to terms with them. It has provided, in the context of the Catholic Church in Ireland, an experience of small group intimacy, with all the closeness and warmth which that entails, which could not possibly be experienced in our large and crowded churches. People got an opportunity to speak about their faith in a safe and secure environment, and to hear others tell what it has meant to them. Many got their first experience of spontaneous prayer in these groups. It also brought a level of enthusiasm into Irish Catholic life and practice which was significant, and, had it been harnessed properly, could have made a difference. All of this is good. But I think that its influence on religious men and women has not been totally positive. At times it has promoted a language and a spirituality, often borrowed from the American Pentecostal Churches, which tended towards a fundamentalist notion of God, and a belief that prayer alone was enough. At its worst it gave a high priority to feelings, as a substitute for solid doctrine, and it had little time for the spirituality of social justice. Often in the charismatic movement it was enough to sing 'Our God reigns' or 'Be not afraid' in the context of a close, emotion-charged group, without addressing the issues that instilled fear and impeded God's reign. The inadequacy of the traditional training of many religious, with its emphasis on piosity rather than theology, made them unable to distinguish what was good from what should have been thrown away in all of this. So its language was often strong on emotion and short on hard-nosed realism. While it has, as I said, been a positive influence in many ways, both to individuals and to the church, one of its negative influences was perhaps to accentuate a move towards soft, woolly, ultimately unreal language.

The same could be said for another movement which flourished for a brief period in the late seventies and early eighties. I refer to Marriage Encounter. This was a movement for married couples, centred around a weekend experience, leading to membership of a loose-knit type of community of those who had done the weekend. It was very American in its language and methods, though brave efforts were made by some people to adapt it to the Irish mentality. It had spectacular success for a short period of years, and then it fell to pieces and collapsed almost overnight. Even though it was specifically for married couples, religious and priests could also do the weekend, and a great many did. Some became very actively involved in the running of the courses, and in the general organisation of the movement. The most obvious outward sign of this movement, and what made it fairly dramatic in the context of our inhibited way of relating in Ireland traditionally, was that it encouraged physical expression of emotions and feelings of love and affection. Within the group all sorts of physical gestures were commonplace – hugging, kissing, holding hands, etc. My first introduction to the movement was a weekend in Belfast, which I did in the company of four other religious and maybe about twenty married couples. When the weekend concluded on Sunday evening it was the custom that a large number of the wider marriage encounter community, those who had done the weekend on previous occasions, would arrive to welcome the new members. (It is interesting to note that it was Belfast, with all the intense bitterness and divisions between the communities, that was the place where Marriage Encounter flourished most.) The place was packed with people, and hugs and kisses were being generously bestowed on all sides by everyone. We five religious had all travelled together from Dublin in one car, and we eventually fought our way through the crowd, carrying our suitcases, and enduring, in the best way possible for inhibited celibate males, this barrage of physical affection. Having arrived at the car we discovered it was blocked in by one of the visitors' cars, which was double-parked. Someone was needed to go back in to make an announcement, and have the offending car removed. But that meant facing into the expressive and expansive crowd once more. A look of consternation appeared on every face, and without saying a word, but understanding perfectly what each one was feeling, we bent down and with a mighty effort lifted the car bodily out of the way!

There were marvellous elements to this movement, and for the while it lasted it helped many marriages. It got husbands and wives talking to one another with an openness that was not common in Irish marriages, and gave them a framework within which to do so. But ultimately, as its rapid collapse demonstrated, it was soft-centred. It didn't have sufficient root in the ordinary reality of life, and the high emotional content made it difficult to control. It was sad to see an organisation that was based on the promotion of love, and which did for a while create a very loving and close atmosphere among its members, collapse with bitterness and division. During its flourishing years I believe it had considerable influence among religious, both in its philosophy and its language. The language of Marriage Encounter became common currency among religious and priests, and its tendency to be soft and emotional had a very detrimental effect on the type of gospel message that was presented at that time.

I have already dealt with the third movement that I believe influenced the language of religious, the self-development movement. Like the other two movements I have mentioned, this one was also very American in its style, and had its own terminology that increasingly became a part of the way religious communicated with each other.

The effects of all of these movements, and of the style of language that developed from them, tended to cocoon religious into an artificial world, separated from the ordinary struggles of people. Communication with the 'outside' world began to decline, and religious life more and more turned in on itself. A study of the documents of Chapters and Assemblies of this era will quickly illustrate that. So much time was spent on internal issues, matters of relationship and organisation within the group. The details of our living together, and the battles over the peripherals which, as I've said, had become the essentials, used up most of our time and energy. Indeed this turning in on ourselves, both as individuals and as groups, was very much a feature of religious life during these years. It is ironic that something that began, after the council, as a great and exciting effort to open up to the world, should end up being so inward looking

Why did it all happen? I believe it was a deliberate, though possibly unconscious, choice by religious. Ultimately it was a failure in courage. It was easier to turn our attention to the internal issues, which at least were relatively clean and comfortable to manage, rather than endeavouring to engage with the issues of an increasingly complex and difficult world, where both our faith, and what our life stood for, were being challenged on all sides. I believe it is also an unconscious response of a group who feel threatened to develop a style of language that cannot easily be understood by those they perceive as threatening them on the outside. This was the era when the first outbreak of anger against the church in Ireland was being ventilated.

I was involved at the time in a form of parish mission apostolate that organised small group discussions in houses. It was an interesting experiment in that it was the first time in this country that Catholics had been brought together with a priest and given the freedom to say whatever they wished about their belief and their church. Generations of hurt got a chance to be expressed, and people took out on individuals the anger they felt against the institution. It was also the time when the debate on contraception was at its height, and resentment at the way the church was seen to be interfering in the private and intimate lives of people was coming out into the open. Working with young people, as so many religious did in those days, was a real challenge. Here, also, anger against the church was common. The apathy of so many of today's youth hadn't yet set in. Religious and priests found themselves regularly on the defensive. They were forced into getting involved in battles and on battle grounds that were not of their own choosing, most

particularly the issues of divorce, abortion and contraception. They
were no longer seen as the unquestioned authority, and were regularly
challenged at a one-to-one level, in small groups, and even occasionally in large settings like public meetings in halls and at church
celebrations. It was very much a new era. A person was no longer
given respect because of the uniform they wore, but instead had to
earn it as an individual. Was it any wonder that at this time so
many religious chose the relatively safe and comfortable haven of
movements like Marriage Encounter, the charismatic movement or
directed retreats, rather than the rough and tumble of trying to
cope with the anger, the questioning, and the confusion of the ordinary Catholic faithful? Some, it must be said, did stay with the
struggle, and are with it to this day, even though age and lack of energy are catching up with them.

It is obvious that in many ways these years were traumatic ones for
religious life. But it is worth saying again that it wasn't only religious life that was experiencing trauma. All the other institutions of
society were undergoing similar upheavals. Marriage and family life
experienced great strain, often similar enough to what religious
were going through.

It is a natural tendency for people, in this type of situation, to look
for ways to escape from the pain of it all. In this chapter I have tried
to highlight two areas that may have been avenues of escape for
some. While it is understandable that these things would happen, it
is important for us now, as we try to assess accurately our current
situation, to be able to identify clearly which trends were positive
and which were not. When we joined many years ago we were told
that we should be faithful to our vocation, and we understood that
in the narrow sense of keeping the vows and saying our prayers.
Today I think we need a very different definition of faithfulness.

CHAPTER 7

The present reality

Recently I was talking on the phone to a religious in her late thirties. I was discussing with her the possibility of attempting a new initiative in the community apostolate. She politely indulged my enthusiasm for a while, but gradually I detected her forced politeness, so I asked her what was wrong. In exasperation she burst out: 'I have just come from the dining-room, where I had dinner with my community. I was the only one in that room under sixty years of age. Would you ever get real, and stop talking about new initiatives!'

The problem of age is one of the most striking things about the present reality in religious life. The statistically average religious in Ireland is rapidly approaching pension age, and looking forward to getting the free travel pass. In terms of energy and enthusiasm for the task, he or she is definitely past their prime. Not that age is the total factor in this. Walter and Albertina Sisulu, the A.N.C. leader from South Africa and his wife, were recent visitors to our country. Walter is eighty-four years of age and Albertina is seventy-nine. Listening to them on the radio I was amazed at their energy. They spoke and thought like two people in the prime of life. It isn't so much your age, as the context in which you are ageing, that seems to make the difference. Clearly the Sisulus are a remarkable couple, but surely the bursting out of new life that has come with the extraordinary changes in their country has given them great vitality. They have lived, and indeed suffered, for this for so long. Now that it has arrived, nothing, not even advancing years, will keep them from savouring it and playing their part. Age in religious life in Ireland works in the opposite way. There are religious of half their age who have less energy and enthusiasm than the Sisulus. When you are in the context of an institution that is itself disintegrating, then the ageing process weighs more heavily on the individual. To remain young in mind and heart while living in an ageing institution is very difficult.

So, the first reality, as I have said, is that the majority of religious are over sixty years of age. They are people who were trained in the forties and the fifties, when the old system was still solidly in place. They have lived through all of the changes. Consequently, there is an immense variety of attitude among them. Some welcomed change as part of the challenge of life. They coped well with it, and grew and developed as individuals through it all. They are lucky people. They have lived exciting and interesting lives, constantly facing and coming to terms with the demands of new situations. They never suffered from boredom! Now in their old age, because of all they have experienced, they are generally rounded and mature people, largely at peace with themselves and the world. In a sense, nothing can surprise them anymore. The Chinese wish, about living in interesting times, has proved for them a blessing rather than a curse.

At the opposite end of the scale are those who were unable to cope with the changes, but who still remained in religious life. Since they could not handle what was happening around them, they used one or other form of escape from reality. Living a life that is, in whatever manner, divorced from reality is not a good preparation for old age. Some of these succumbed to alcoholism, or some other form of addiction. Others clung desperately to the old style piosity and acted as if nothing had changed. Others became bitter, hard people, sour with life and with humanity in general. They have become crotchety, difficult old people, who are a poor advertisement for the life they have lived. Any religious reading this will, I'm sure, be able to think of people who fit fairly well into the two extremes I have outlined. But, as is the manner of life generally, the majority of older religious fit somewhere in between the two extremes.

That generation can be considered to be lucky in one important factor. While they have seen the rapid decline of the system, it still survives well enough to give them security and care in their old age. That can not be said with any degree of certainty for those coming immediately behind them. I refer to religious in their middle years, those from the mid-forties to the mid-fifties. These now represent the last generation of the boom times for religious life. Consequently there are still many of them around.

Despite their numbers, they represent only a remnant of those who started out in the sixties. In their early years of training, the initial exodus from seminaries and convents had begun, and they experienced the departure of many of their classmates and good friends. It was upsetting at first, but gradually they got used to it, and it became a part of life. When the changes came after the council they were young and resilient, and they greeted them with enthusiasm. They had great hopes for a renewed church and a style of religious life that would be relevant to the modern world. It was in the excitement and promise of this time, in the early to mid-seventies, that most of them made their final commitment at profession or ordination. The early years were good. They had the freedom to live a more open way of life, and to bring freshness and originality to their apostolates. Gradually they began to experience the fading of their hopes for a bright future. Instead they saw the church turning in on itself, and pulling back from any serious engaging with the modern world. Attitudes which they thought they had left permanently behind began to re-emerge. The long-drawn out debate on contraception, and later the position adopted by the church in the debates on social issues in our society, were a big disappointment to some. They had come firmly to believe in the freedom of the individual conscience, but now they saw the church adopting the position, 'Yes, but only if your conscience agrees with our teachings'. They discovered that the new approach to sexuality which they had learned in theology, emphasising in a positive way the goodness and beauty of it, was only skin deep in the church, and that the old negative attitudes, and the desire to control the private lives of people, were still strong. Issues of social justice had become important to them in their youth, but they saw the Vatican adopting an antagonistic attitude to liberation theology, and silencing theologians. In recent years another wave of departures has happened among this age-group. Middle-aged religious have been leaving, not so much because they have difficulties with faith or celibacy, or that they want to get married, but simply because they want to free themselves from what they see as the unbearable burden of a decaying institution. Some of them claim that the only way they can continue to live by their original ideals is to break away from their particular institution, since they see it as having become much too focused on self-preservation.

This middle-aged group are now the ones who are trying to keep the show on the road. They are in the positions of authority in their institutes; at least those of them who are still willing to accept these positions. Increasingly people are opting out and no longer making themselves available for any such post. This is not surprising, since being in authority in religious life today is a dreadfully difficult and frustrating task. When a religious community has been in a town or a city for some considerable period of time, they usually become an important feature of the place. They build up their apostolate over the years, and provide a service to the people. In response, the people have usually been generous to the community. But they have also developed certain expectations. When this apostolate was built up the community was large in numbers, with many young and energetic members. Now the same commitments, and the same expectations from the people, are trying to be met by a community that is much reduced in personnel, and almost all over sixty years of age. This makes for an impossible situation, the burden of which tends to fall on the person in charge, who no longer has the power to demand that individual members do a particular task. This is more of a problem for the male communities, especially the orders of priests. Religious priests running a church, which may or may not have a parish attached, depended on the donations of the people for their livelihood. In consequence they feel more under pressure to continue to provide a service, even if they no longer have the personnel to do it properly. They are not as free to pack their bags and move out of the place. If, for instance, the monastery has collected half a million pounds twenty years ago to repair the roof of the church, they cannot easily decide to close that same church today. People often have great affection for their local religious church, sometimes seeing it as a shrine, a holy place. And that affection can have a tradition of generations behind it. Maybe their grandparents donated the altar or something. In other words, the very success of the religious community in that town or area in the past, and the affection in which they are held by the people, makes their present position more difficult to manage.

Up to now, most of the clerical religious orders have not faced up to this problem, and instead have tried to keep going as best they can. That is why we see so many religious churches around the country still functioning. But mostly they are staffed by a small group of old men, often quite traditional in their mentality. The service they are able to offer is only a pale shadow of what it once was, and their declining congregations are inevitably made up increasingly of the older people. This small community is often still living in a large, usually nineteenth-century, monastery, more than twice the size of what they require, and very expensive to run. Most of our larger cities have a number of these churches and communities situated close to each other around the centre of the city. The people have moved out to the suburbs, and the area around them is mostly non-residential, consisting of shops and offices. They compete with each other for a smaller market.

Religious women, mainly because they worked in schools and hospitals and were paid by the state, were more independent. Consequently they have made much greater progress in getting rid of the large old convents and moving into smaller, often purpose-built units, more suited to their numbers and their age. It is easier to withdraw from a school or a hospital. Lay people can be put in place of the religious, and the service remains. But if religious priests pull out of a big city centre church, it closes.

The middle-aged religious can often be faced with personal dilemmas also. They joined a thriving institution, and now they see it in
terminal decline. As a person moves on in life it is important for
their sense of well-being to feel that their life has been worthwhile,
that their passing through this world has made a difference, and
that they have made some type of contribution that was significant,
even in a small way. There is no pleasure, in your middle years, to
be surrounded by structural decay and death. How can you preserve your own morale, and your belief in the value of this life, in
the midst of all of this?

Of course not every religious believes that the institution is dying.
Some hold on to the strong conviction that there is a future; very
different, and much smaller in numbers than the past, but a future
none the less, and something worth living for and working towards. They give their energy to doing what they can to shape and
assist this new model of religious life for the new age. Others, particularly those who have worked for some time on the foreign missions, see things in a more global sense, and say that while religious
life might be dying in Ireland, and even in the western world, it is
thriving in other areas, most notably in Africa, parts of South
America, the Far East, and some countries in the old communist
block. They talk of the day when missionaries will come from these
countries to repay and old debt, and re-convert Ireland to the
Christian faith!

In this context, it has to be noted that there are serious questions
being asked by missionaries about the large numbers of vocations
to religious life in some parts of the third world, and the way in
which some of the declining congregations from Europe and
America are setting up communities in these countries, and fairly
quickly beginning to take vocations. It would appear that some
areas, especially in Africa, are experiencing a situation somewhat
similar to what I described earlier of the Ireland of the forties and
the fifties, when very large numbers were entering seminaries and
convents here. The same questions arise about the motivation of
the candidates who apply, since becoming a religious in some poorer

countries can be a major step up the social ladder, both in terms of status and comfort. There is a worry that congregations which are mainly western in origin and personnel, but who quickly accept large numbers of Africans, without being in a position to do proper screening and give the necessary quality of training, may be reaping a whirlwind.

There is another group of religious who do not seem to concern themselves about the state of religious life at all. They seem to carry on their lives as if everything was going normally, and the future was secure and certain. I'm sure some of these are people for whom the reality is too painful to face or too personally unsettling, and this is their way of coping. Others have settled into a comfortable existence. As I've said elsewhere, religious life today does offer comfort to those who wish to avail of it. With a weakened authority system, rarely are people confronted about their lifestyle anymore. The system provides for great material security. Whether or not a person does a day's work, there will still be three meals put on the table in front of him or her each day. A person can afford to be idle without having to suffer the consequences. I often wonder what effect this situation has on the overall quality of life of the community.

Others have decided to go their own way, probably recognising that, in the midst of the collapse all around them, the best attitude is self-preservation. They have undergone re-training for some form of personal project and have set up an individual apostolate. This individual apostolate may have no relation to the general work of the congregation. In order to give recognition to their work, the notion of the charism of the founder or foundress becomes gradually so stretched that it can include almost anything. While most of these religious still live in the community, they do their own thing. They can be very hard-working, and often quite successful. Religious orders have always had a small number of these types of people, but as the number increases fragmentation is accelerated.

'I wish I was twenty years younger!' a religious in her fifties said to me recently. 'If I was I would be gone in the morning!' It is hard to

know how many feel like this. But it is not surprising that some
would. They may have ten to twenty years of active life ahead of
them, and when they look into the future it is not an encouraging
prospect. At its worst it could involve a small number of people de-
voting most of their energy to some of the following:

– Caring for large groups of infirm men/women, until one joins
the group oneself.

– Closing long-established apostolates, and trying to deal with
the resultant disappointment and even anger of the people who
availed of these services.

– Closing, and attempting to sell, large convents and monasteries.

– Dealing with teachers, nurses, unions and government de-
partments in trying to off-load schools and hospitals.

– Coping with fellow-religious whose lives have disintegrated
due to their inability to face what is happening.

– Most disturbing of all, moving the bodies of the dead from
the community cemetery as the convent or monastery is sold. (I
wonder how necessary this is. Surely it should only be done as a
last resort, and never in order to increase the value of the property being sold.)

In this context there is a real danger of disillusionment, a sense that
life has played a nasty trick, landing the person in this situation
when they are too old to make a fresh start. There is no doubt that
many individuals are feeling the pressure. As they try to sustain
with smaller numbers the traditional commitments, overwork becomes a problem for some. As people lose faith and hope in the future they can suffer one or other form of breakdown. Any religious
superior today would tell you that they spend a great deal of their
time with individuals whose lives are falling apart. Society in general
is less sympathetic and supportive to religious life. Indeed many regard it as eccentric and even unhealthy. It is important that if a religious
of whatever age gets to the stage where they can no longer cope,
every assistance should be given to them, both personal and financial, to enable them to start a new life outside of the institution, if

that is what they wish. And yet many are still working away quietly, giving great service in different areas of Irish life. They deserve immense admiration and respect. Despite the difficult realities that they face, both within their congregations and in society at large, they continue to work steadily from day to day, and give witness as best they can to the God in whom they believe.

There is a small number of younger religious, and by that I mean people under forty years of age. For those of them who are reflecting on life at all, it has to be very difficult. The future must look very insecure. From my experience they are a varied group of people. For many the notion of a life-long commitment is a bit unreal, so that they tend to be here for the present, and very open to where their lives might go. In this they are typical of their contemporaries generally, who often have the same attitude to other life-long commitments, like marriage. Community life can be difficult for them because they are usually living with people who are old enough to be their parents, or even their grandparents, and with maybe one, or none at all, of their own age-group. An understandable tendency in that situation is to find their friendships and their support outside the community. This means that often, while living in the community, they spend as little time there as possible. That creates its own problems, and it is not surprising that a good number are leaving. But also, there are some of that age-group who have developed very conservative attitudes in matters of theology, if not in life-style, and fit much too comfortably into the system. They have reverted to the authoritarianism of an older age, and are almost like people out of their time.

The fact that younger religious are so few in number and that a great many of their contemporaries in society at large have ceased to practice their religion or even become unbelievers, must inevitably effect them. As distinct from the generations that went before them, they are much more likely to suffer, not just from doubts about the meaning of the life or the value of celibacy, but from real doubts about the faith itself. All in all, considering how few there are, and the instability among them, it is hard to see how one could argue convincingly that they will succeed in re-shaping this way of life, and passing it on to future generation.

There are few, and in the case of some congregations none at all, new members coming through to augment the declining personnel of religious communities. There has been a steady reduction in numbers of postulants to almost all orders during the last thirty years. With the introduction of free education and the opening up of opportunities for young people in Ireland and abroad, less people want to become priests and religious. The calibre of person applying has tended to change also. In the old days many of the most able were drawn to religious life because it gave opportunity for living a challenging life. Through the seventies and the eighties these were more inclined to choose other professions, and religious life attracted many who were not only less able, but also insecure and looking for some shelter from the difficult world in which they were growing up. After a short time, these found that religious life was not immune from the difficulties facing the world at large, and could not provide them with the safe environment for which they were searching, so they left. That, I believe, goes some way towards explaining why, during these years, fairly large numbers were still joining, but almost all of them departed after a few years. There are very few who wish to become religious now. The scandals in the church have added to the problem, so that what was a trickle has almost dried up entirely.

In this context, it is worth noting that a small number of very traditional congregations, who have retained a formation system similar to the pre-council times, are still getting some applicants. Their methods of training are held in some suspicion by society at large, who consider their closed and very protective style of formation to be similar to the brain-washing and 'love-bombing' of the cults. What they are in fact doing is simply using the system that was prevalent in all religious orders up until the nineteen sixties. While some ultra-conservative people within the church often use the fact that these congregations are getting recruits as support for their overall position, the phenomenon is of too small a scale and at too early a stage to draw any definite conclusions. Because of their highly structured system, these congregations are in danger of attracting the insecure type of young person I mentioned above, who finds living in such a rapidly changing world as we have today too difficult, and who is looking for shelter. One of the clear lessons we have learned from the past is not to be blinded by numbers. The number of people who are drawn to an idea has nothing to do with its inherent validity. There have been a great many people who joined religious life down through the centuries for a variety of reasons that had little or nothing to do with a call from God.

How has the system coped with all these developments? Systems, as is their nature, continue to operate and cope as best they can. People are duly elected and appointed to all the various positions, and they serve their terms of office. Efforts are being made to try to face the reality of the situation. Seminars, chapters and assemblies have been held. Documents have been produced. It is hard to see what effect, if any, they have had, and yet they continue unabated. As time goes by, the content of the policy documents bears less and less relation to the reality on the ground. Discussion has become a substitute for action, mainly because most people are at a loss as to what action to take that would have any real effect on the situation.

In a sense, there are two levels at work. At the official level, things are being discussed and committees set up to attempt to deal with them. But at the level of the ordinary individual, people are carrying on their lives, effectively ignoring the latest policy documents or position papers. Sometimes they don't even read them. They have seen too many documents over the years, and no longer believe that they will make any difference. In fact many do not want them to make a difference, because it would involve too much disturbance, and they are too settled for that. Yet they pretend to give allegiance and support to all of the efforts. As a consequence, there is a strong sense of unreality about a lot of what is happening.

An interesting development is that in some institutes a move towards centralisation is taking place, with new and complex structures of national government being formed in place of traditional regional units, and power once again moving away from the individual towards the centre. The effort, energy and money being put into the setting up of these structures, at a time when the future is so uncertain, is hard to understand. It would appear from the outside to be an exercise similar to rearranging the deck-chairs on the Titanic, or a desperate attempt to convince oneself that new structures can bring new life. But the problem is much deeper than this. New structures will not restore the spirit of an institute, or give new life to a system that is dying.

Traditionally, religious in Ireland were not well off. They lived frugally, and whatever spare money they had was ploughed back into their work, or into building new convents and monasteries to cater for their increasing numbers. Now things have changed. Numbers are declining, and religious find themselves in possession of large properties which they no longer require. While often the buildings are too old and unwieldy to be of much use, the sites on which they are situated can make them very valuable. How can people, vowed to a life of poverty, deal adequately with this type of situation? So far, the property has mostly been sold to the highest bidder, and the money invested wisely with the help of finance companies. As a consequence, religious investments are large, and increasing. This is being justified for the following reason. Religious communities, as I've said, are mostly made up of elderly people. Their earning power is limited, and caring for them properly, especially if they become invalids, can be very expensive. Over the next thirty years or so, religious communities will have large expenses and little income. They need to use wisely the money they get from selling their buildings so that they can properly care for all the elderly members. Money management has become much more sophisticated and is now following the dictates of professional financiers. As a rule, the individual communities no longer lodge their money with the local bank. Instead it is whipped away immediately to a centralised place where it can be invested overnight and produce maximum dividend. This makes excellent economic sense. It could be said that in this whole area, religious have become wise in the ways of the world. They are no longer the 'soft touch' that they often were in the past. But it could equally be argued, with some justification, that all of this careful and sensible husbanding of money is another indication of a loss of spirit, or maybe even a loss of faith in the Person who told us to learn from the lilies of the field, and not to worry about tomorrow. By carefully building up a nest-egg to secure our future, we can hardly consider ourselves to be acting in a counter-cultural way.

This is an outline of some aspects of the present reality as I see it. It is not an easy time to be a religious. To be living in a time of decline is far more difficult than a time of growth and expansion. I believe that the people who oversee the death of a religious congregation are much more deserving of the title of saint that those who started it. When I have written or spoken like this in recent years, some religious tell me that I am too pessimistic, that things are not quite so bad, that there is more hope for the future. Maybe they are correct, but it seems to me that the evidence, as I have tried to outline it in this book, is strongly in support of my conclusions.

Others question my lack of faith. They quote from the scriptures: 'When I am weak, then I am strong,' or 'Unless the grain of wheat falls into the ground and dies it remains a grain, but if it dies it bears much fruit.' There is a great danger that texts like these can be used to anaesthetise ourselves in the face of the present reality. But what if we really took the texts seriously? Maybe they would urge us into accepting, even embracing, failure and death as the world sees them. We might throw in our lot with the poor by becoming one with them, and ceasing to husband our large investments. Christ said to the rich young man: 'Go, sell what you have ... and you will have treasure in heaven.' We cannot have it both ways. We cannot use the words of Christ to comfort us in our difficulties while at the same time lacking the religious will to forego our earthly treasures. Could it be said that the ultimate call to renewal was too much for us?

CHAPTER 8

A time for courage

I will begin this final chapter of the book by looking briefly at the question of what is the fundamental purpose, the essential core, of religious life. There are at present, and have been down through the history of the church, so many different forms of religious life, that it is not easy to find a definition to cover them all adequately. However, trying to sum it up in one sentence, I would say that the fundamental purpose of living the form of life we call religious life is first and foremost the pursuit of the search for God. Immediately this raises the question; is not the search for God the ultimate purpose of all Christian living? Of course it is. It could even be argued that searching for God, in the sense of engaging with and trying to throw some light on the mystery of life, is a task in which the whole of humanity is in some sense engaged. But the religious devotes him or herself to it in a special way. They choose a style of life that frees them to some extent from the pressure and distraction of the world, so that they will be more available to the task of discovering God. They could be said to be in the vanguard of a task that engages all human beings to a greater or lesser extent. It is their function to be able to light the way, at least partially, for people who are so weighed down by the pressures of living that they have little time for this quest.

The second purpose of religious life follows from the first. Using theological language, we say that religious are meant to be an eschatological sign of the kingdom of God. What this means is that, by the way they live and the values they proclaim, religious are a sign, or give a witness, to the fact that there is a life greater than this one, an eternal life, known in Christian terms as the kingdom of God. It is in this context, and as part of this sign, that the taking of vows like poverty and celibacy begins to make some sense. Essential to this sign or witness is a life that is lived simply, devoid of worldly ambition, and devoted to the service of humanity.

These twin purposes, searching for God and being a sign of the kingdom, are common to all forms of consecrated religious life. Some congregations or institutes take on a third purpose. They come together for a particular task, for example, to educate the children of the poor, or, as is the case with my own congregation, to preach the gospel to the most abandoned. Congregations who focus on a particular task are known as *apostolic* religious congregations, and they are the most common type of religious orders in the church. The congregations that were set up solely for the first two purposes are known as *contemplative* orders.

One of the interesting aspects of what is happening in religious life today is that the contemplative orders seem to be better able, in a sense, to ride the storm of the present time, and retain their meaning. I believe this has to do with the fact that their purpose is so fundamental and so rooted in the meaning of life and human existence. One could say that their purpose is global and enduring. The apostolic orders, on the other hand, are rooted in a particular task at a particular time. As religious they also took on the search for God and the witness to his kingdom, but they never became totally focused on them. They tried to be apostolic and contemplative at the same time. It is possible to be a contemplative, apostolic person, to infuse one's actions with the spirit of God. However, the church had really only one model for religious life, the monastic model, and so, apostolic religious were forced to live their lives in a mould which gave primacy to the contemplative and never really integrated the apostolic – it was merely tagged on to the contemplative, and holiness was equated with the quantity of one's prayer rather than with the quality of one's actions. So we had people who tried to be 'Carthusians at home and apostles abroad'. No wonder it never really worked.

My contention in this book is that the form of religious life that we know as apostolic religious is in terminal decline in this country, and possibly even in the whole western world. I am not suggesting that religious life in general will die out. It has a tradition going right back to the early days of the church, and undoubtedly it will survive in one form or another. Contemplative religious life will certainly remain with us. But some new way of life needs to be found for those who come together to meet a particular apostolic need within the church. The way that we have known has failed to adapt to the modern world, and consequently is out of its time and has to die out. In the course of this book I have outlined my reasons for coming to this conclusion, and tried to discover what were the aspects of the traditional way of living this life that made it incapable of the sort of change that was required. I have also tried to pinpoint why some of the major efforts at adaptation failed, to the extent that they did not point the way to the future. Maybe apostolic religious life is dying because it was a flawed product.

Already in our time, other agencies have emerged who are doing some of the work that traditionally was done by religious, and in many cases they are attracting the people who in past generations became religious. These agencies are living proof that a person can serve suffering humanity without becoming religious. They don't have to undergo a long period of training, take vows, make a life commitment, or be in any way set apart from their peers. It is hard to say whether or not this development has hastened the decline of apostolic religious life, or is a consequence of it. In any case, the two have gone on side by side since the early sixties.

The first example of this is the Aid Agencies, most especially *Concern*, *Trócaire* and *Goal*. A great many young Irish people join one or other of these agencies and go to work in the third world for periods of time, anything from a few months to a few years. The sort of inspiration or generosity that in the past led people to want to work in the foreign missions and help the poor is now being siphoned off into this form of activity. It has a great appeal for today's young person. Instead of enduring long years of preparation, if the person has some form of qualification or skill that is useful in a situation of poverty, they can be in the thick of the action with one of the agencies within a few months.

With the advancement of social services in most countries in the western world, the state is now looking after many of the tasks for which religious were founded in the past, particularly education, health care and social services. As I've said in a previous chapter when the changes came religious lost the sense of being different, more special or holier than ordinary people. It is natural that a young person who wants to become a teacher, nurse or social worker, would find it difficult to see the point of becoming a religious when they could do the exact same work equally well as a lay person.

Most religious congregations were founded to, in one way or another, help the poor. As I've said, during the first half of this century they became increasingly middle-class. It is interesting to look at who is working among the poor in our society today. There are undoubtedly some religious involved, but they tend to be involved more as individuals or as small groups rather than as whole congregations. Organisations like the Simon Community are more clearly identified with this type of work, and as a consequence they tend to attract the very idealistic young.

As well as the blurring of lines between religious and lay people, as I mentioned earlier, the distinction between religious and secular priests is also fading. One of the reasons for this is the taking over and running of parishes by religious. This has happened increasingly in the past twenty years. Two things have contributed to it. Firstly, as the traditional charism of some congregations, meaning the task for which they were originally founded, either became too difficult or was no longer possible, it was an easy option for them to take on parishes in the vicinity of their public churches. Some deliberately chose to take on parishes in poor areas. Secondly, with the shortage of diocesan priests, bishops were glad to have religious who were willing to run parishes. It eased the pressure for them. But by blurring the distinction between the religious and the secular priest, it lessened the distinctiveness of being religious.

In the face of all this decline, what are we to do about new applicants, because there are still some who wish to join religious congregations? Most congregations are open to accepting new members, and, if the candidate succeeds in passing whatever form of assessment is used, they are invited in. The systems of formation are now very varied, with different institutes having developed in different ways over recent years. Some groups, because their numbers are so small, have got together to form a joint formation system. The average length of time between entry and either final profession or ordination is somewhere between eight and ten years. These years are mostly spent in study, with maybe one or two years of experience in some more direct form of apostolic work. As I've said elsewhere, the fall-out rate during these years of training is very high. Many young people find them too long. They also have great difficulty with the notion of making a life-long commitment to one profession. In today's world, with everything changing so rapidly, and with people moving quickly from one job to another and often from one relationship to another, being willing to stick at one thing for a person's whole life is more difficult than ever before.

The question of taking new members needs to be urgently looked at. Of all the dilemmas facing religious today, this is the biggest one. How long more can we justify taking recruits to our congregations? Is it fair to young people to take them in, even if they wish to join, at this present time? With the large majority of religious over fifty years of age, and the average for most congregations well into the sixties, how could a person in their late teens or early twenties be expected to settle in and feel at home? With the extraordinary rate of change that we have experienced in the past thirty years, the gap between a person in their teens and a person is their sixties is the equivalent of many generations. There are not enough religious in the intervening age brackets to bridge the gap properly or effectively. Consequently I believe that the time has come when we need to face the fact that we should not take any more young people into our way of life. Why invite young people into a way of life that is so obviously declining? Surely it is placing an impossible burden on them.

This is the most difficult and painful question for any institution to have to face. Its natural instinct is to preserve itself, and the members within it need the assurance that there will be a future to give meaning to their own lives. Who wants to see the way of life, which they have believed in and given themselves to so completely, die out with them? There is also the natural desire to have someone coming along to look after you in your old age. If our generation of religious give up on the possibility of a future, and stop taking recruits, then we face an uncertain prospect. How would it be possible for us to preserve any sort of morale among ourselves? Even to begin to ask the question about whether we are entitled to take any more new members is in itself a blow to morale, and could so easily become a self-fulfilling prophecy. And yet, not to ask it is to fly in the face of an ever more obvious reality.

Some among us would argue that, while religious life is in serious decline, it is not terminal. They suggest that this way of life will survive, with much smaller numbers and in a very different form from what we have known. Consequently they argue for the continued acceptance of new members, because it will be they, with help and support from existing members, who will shape the new future. By closing our doors to new members, they assert, we lose hope in a very real future, and we betray the style of life to which we are committed.

I do not accept this reading of the situation. I agree that something new will surely develop, but I do not think that it is the necessary pattern of life that the new comes from the embers of the old. I believe that what is old and tired has to die, and that new growth will come from other sources, sometimes very surprising ones. The tired earth needs rest; it needs the fallow period in order to renew itself. Then it must be ploughed, harrowed and manured, so that a renewed earth can be ready to receive the new seed, and the new roots can go deep into the soil. In a way, the desperate clinging to life of the old can be an obstacle to new growth. The weeds of yesteryear need to be cleared away with the harrow in order to make space for the spring crop.

Many of our existing religious orders have lasted a long time. Like the oak tree they have stood strong and tall, weathering the centuries. The wonder is, not that they have grown old, but that they have survived so long. Now I believe they have become too set in their ways, and too turned in on themselves, to give the freedom and support necessary for something new to develop. In many instances, like the weeds in the ground, they have become expert at blocking anything that is new and different. Their declining state has led to many of them becoming entrenched and defensive in their attitudes, and they see efforts at something new as a threat to be resisted.

The style of religious life that I have been writing about, religious who are devoted to a specific task in the church, could be said to have become a significant feature of church life in the Middle Ages. Since then it has faced and overcome many challenges. It survived the Renaissance and the Reformation. It even recovered from the suppression of the monasteries by Henry VIII, though that was a significant setback at the time. It also survived the French Revolution and the Enlightenment of the 19th century. I have given my reasons why I believe it was unable to survive the challenge of this present era. It had become too solidified, too inflexible. And yet a tantalising question remains in my mind. Would it have battled its way through this era also if it had not been undermined from within by the Second Vatican Council? It had weathered many a storm, and had become expert at coping with external enemies of all sorts. What it could not handle was the approval given by the church at the highest level to the notions of freedom and personal responsibility.

So the last challenge presenting itself to us, the religious of my era, is, I believe, to face up to and plan for an orderly demise. In a sense it is the greatest challenge of all. The first step will be the decision not to accept any more new members. Having done that it will be important for us not to sink into despair, but to continue to find a reason for living this way of life in our time. We must plan carefully for the disposal of our property. We cannot allow ourselves to be too greatly influenced by the financial experts in the management of our money, never forgetting that, of their nature, they work from a very different value system from us. We must resist the temptation to hoard money in order to secure our comfort in old age, but instead place at least some trust in the providence of the God in whom we believe. So the careful dispersing of some of our investments needs to be attended to. For international congregations, with thriving units in other, maybe poorer, parts of the world, whether the money be given to them, or be used here among the people from whom it was obtained in the first place, is a matter for debate. I personally, would like to see us giving much greater financial support to lay people who wish to be involved more fully in the church. The future would appear to be with them, but unless the church is willing to give them proper financial remuneration they will not be able to survive.

Finally, we need to have great trust in God. We need to realise that in the mystery at work in life no institution, religious or secular, is essential. God works in strange and unpredictable ways. The world went on before our foundation and, after us, life will continue. The gospel will be preached by a new generation in new and appropriate ways, and the plan of God will work its way towards its fulfilment in the kingdom. We can learn from Robert Browning:

> Grow old along with me!
> The best is yet to be,
> The last of life, for which the first was made
> Our times are in his hands
> Who saith, A whole I planned,
> Youth shows but half; trust God: see all, nor be afraid.